PRESSING FORWARD

PRESSING FORWARD

*Pushing Through Fear and Anxiety
to Find My Truest Self*

APRIL POYNTER

WordCrafts

Pressing Forward
Pushing Through Fear and Anxiety to Find My Truest Self
Copyright © 2017
April Poynter

Front cover concept by Tony Poynter
Author photo by Katherine Michael | Voyage Creatives Photography
Cover design by Jonathan Grisham

Published by WordCrafts Press
Buffalo, WY 82834
www.wordcrafts.net

CONTENTS

DEDICATION

This book is dedicated to my husband, Tony.
You are a man of action married to a woman who loves words.
You're steady and still while I tear up the world. Thank you
for letting me fly freely even when you don't understand an
intuitive-feeling, right-brain creative.

To Trinity, my beloved.
You are the reason I kept living during my season of deep
rooted anxiety and depression. I'm grateful for you and your
explosive excitement for life.

To Sway, my "always little" baby.
You live life outside the box. I admire you tremendously. You
have taught me so much more in your four years of life than
I could have ever learned on my own.

INTRODUCTION

There was a long pause as I sat in the car with the phone up to my ear. I felt so much anxiety fill my body.

"That's exactly it, Tony," I said to my husband as excitement and fear jolted through me. "We say we'll do whatever and go wherever to bring hope and healing to others. We say we'll go wherever God wants to send us and yet we hold on to our safety post. We allow Him to navigate our lives as long as we get to hold on to our safety post. Yesterday I prayed that God would open me up and remove anything that's not from Him. I asked Him to remove anything that's hindering me. I know He's saying it's time to let go. I'm pressing forward, babe."

Tony was silent. So was I.

I had devoted my life to Jesus for five years at this point. I was head over heels in love. I was all in.

I had a cold. I had been coughing my head off for two weeks and about to see the doctor. There were a few minutes left to wrap up my conversation before my appointment. I took a wheezy breath, coughed, and said, "I don't want this safety or control anymore. I'm letting go."

~

I got fired from my job. I had only worked there for three months. Everything was going great until I decorated my office and put a photo of my, at the time, three-year-old daughter on the desk.

My boss walked by to see the decor and scoped out the picture. "Your daughter is cute," he said. "She's so brown. Is your husband brown?"

'What the...?' I thought. I'm sure my face portrayed exactly what I was thinking.

"Are you asking me if my daughter is biracial?"

"Yes," he said.

I responded, "She is biracial."

"Oh, cool. She's cute," he said.

From that day forward my boss stopped talking to me. We had connected so well since I had started working there. We had daily meetings. And now, he was saying nothing to me and avoiding me at all costs. A coworker shared that he was racist, but I didn't believe it. He just didn't seem like the racist type. But something was definitely off. I confronted him head-on.

"Are you treating me different because my husband is black and I'm white?"

He acted appalled. "How dare you ask me that?"

"I'm just asking. You have not been the same toward me ever since you saw the picture of Trinity on my desk and found out she was biracial. What changed?"

"Nothing. I'm just busy," he said.

The next day he fired me.

Oh, sorry. He "laid me off."

This is what sparked my conversation with my husband about letting go and trusting God even when we couldn't understand. I was still processing the termination and the grounds for termination. I was told it was because my role and the Director of Operations' role were pretty much the same thing, there was no need for both of us. I had been married to Tony for six years, and to my knowledge had never experienced discrimination for being in an interracial relationship.

Prior to this job, I had been a stay at home mom for six months after being let go from a company that was literally shut down by the IRS and FBI for fraud, money laundering, and a lot of other stuff you hear about in the news, but never really ever happens to you. Well, it happened to me.

I had left a job of five years for this great opportunity, just to get five months in and have the FBI raid my place of employment. All of us employed by this particular company learned we had no health benefits, even though premiums had been coming out of our pay checks, and that we were all terminated - effective immediately - because the company didn't exist anymore.

Yeah, so that happened.

Six months after being unemployed, my husband and I decided it was time for me to go back to work to help our family financially. I went back to work just to get "laid off" three months later because my daughter was brown. On top of the stresses that come along with being unemployed and the grief of discrimination, I had this stupid cold that wouldn't go away.

~

I hung up the phone with my husband, and just sat in the car for another minute. I felt peace about letting go. I didn't want to just say that God was Lord over my life; I wanted to actually let Him be Lord over my life and let Him lead me.

I went into my appointment and shared my concerns about my cough and chest congestion. What happened next stopped my life completely for the next year, and altered me forever. The doctor did her routine vitals check. You know the drill;

"Open your mouth, stick out your tongue, say, aaahh." I figured she would feel my glands, check my blood pressure, write a prescription and I'd head home. She did all the routine checks, but when she checked my blood pressure, a confused look crossed her face.

"Hm," she said. "Let me see your other arm."

I stretched out my left arm and she checked my blood pressure, again. She looked perplexed.

"Your blood pressure is really high," she said. "We'll want to keep an eye on that."

She then told me I had a virus and it would need to run its course. I walked out of the office. As the door closed behind me a single thought was stuck in my mind; "Your blood pressure is really high."

I had never been told anything was wrong with me. Ever. In fact, I had worked very hard to please and perfect just to avoid anyone ever telling me something was wrong with me in regard to any and all areas of my life.

I pondered what it could mean as I stood outside in the parking lot digging my keys out of my purse. I drove to the daycare to pick my daughter up, when I realized I didn't have a snack or juice for her - an absolute necessity for a peaceful ride home. I stopped by the Rite-Aid near her daycare. As I skimmed the junk snack aisle, trying to decide between Gold Fish or Doritos, I suddenly felt like I couldn't breathe. The more I tried to catch my breath, the harder it was to breathe. My vision grew hazy. I felt as though I would black out. I threw down the Gold Fish and Doritos, ran out of the store and sat on a bench nearby.

My heart was racing. My palms were sweating. I was shaking and still having a hard time breathing. I called my husband

and told him something was wrong with me and I needed to go home immediately. I could not get our daughter from school. Something was seriously wrong. He agreed to pick our daughter up and told me to go home and rest.

I drove home. It was the longest and scariest ride ever. I kept feeling as though I would black out. I couldn't get home fast enough. I was so scared but eventually made it home. I ran up the steps to our apartment, threw my bags on the floor, ran to the bedroom and buried myself in the bed. I was afraid to move. I found a sense of calm again, but was afraid if I moved this crazy thing would start happening again.

It would have been nice to have a friend I could call, who might offer some comfort, but I was in a season of life where my relationships were broken. All of my old friends seemed stuck in the past. I had to decide if I was going to stay where they were, or move on without them. I'd had enough of their drama, back-biting and small-mindedness. I had broken those ties months earlier. Now I was on my own.

I tried to watch a movie to find relief, but it was no use. I was so overstimulated that the tiniest details of the movie overwhelmed me. It wasn't even a new movie. I'd watched it before. Why was this so hard?

Tony came home and found me huddled in the bedroom. He hugged me close to him.

"Are you okay?" he asked.

"I don't know what happened. The doctor told me I had a virus, that I was okay, but my blood pressure was high. I was fine, and then I got really ill and felt weird. I thought I was having a heart attack."

Tony suggested I try to rest. I laid there for a while with my mind racing all over the place. Eventually I fell asleep.

The next day I woke up and felt fine. I was so relieved to be back to normal. I just wanted to get my day started by taking my daughter to daycare. I had told her I'd take her by the local bakery and get her a muffin.

Trinity and I went to the bakery and waited in line as we scouted the breakfast pastries. Standing there, it happened again. My heart started beating fast. I felt faint. I began to freak out. Fear overwhelmed me. I was afraid of... something. But there was nothing to be afraid of.

I somehow managed to hold it together long enough to get through ordering and paying for our pastries without looking like a complete lunatic, but it wasn't easy. It didn't help that the cashier and her coworkers chose this particular moment to comment on how beautiful my daughter was.

Her hair is so amazing! What a sweet personality! How old is she?

Can't they see I was freaking out? I thought as I fake-smiled back at them. *Stop talking to my kid! Give me my carbs and leave us alone.*

They eventually let up, I snatched the pastry bag from the cashier's hand and made a mad dash to my car. I burst out crying and called my husband. "I'm dying. Something is wrong with me!"

"Okay. I hear you, April," he tried to talk me down off the ledge. "I've been through something similar before. Go to the hospital. I'll meet you there."

I managed to drop my daughter off at daycare and made it to the hospital. I felt safe with my husband, but I felt safer being at the hospital. I told the nurse at reception I was having chest pains and trouble breathing. She placed a red piece of paper on my clipboard chart and told me someone would be with me shortly. Apparently, the red paper clipboards get priority. I was called back almost immediately.

My vitals were taken. All were okay.

An EKG was performed. All was well.

The doctor examined me. He told me I was fine.

That should all be incredibly encouraging, right? But it wasn't encouraging. It was discouraging. I was not fine. I was not well. I was not okay!

"I don't feel fine," I told the doctor. I felt fine two days ago. I'm not fine now. This doesn't feel like fine."

"All your tests say you're fine," he answered. "Your blood work says you're fine. Your EKG says you're fine. You're fine." He gave me a doctorly pat on the shoulder and explained, "I think you've just become very aware of what's going on around you and in you. There's like this curtain in your mind that keeps you from being overstimulated. It keeps you from feeling your shirt on your skin, or your shoes on your feet. Your curtain has just opened up a bit wider, so You're taking in more sensory input than normal. It's normal that you might feel overwhelmed. But trust me ... You're fine."

That's what he left me with.

"You're fine."

I took his word for it. I left the hospital and drove back home. I was tired. I was scared. I was defeated. I was numb. But I wasn't fine.

Days went by and I still wasn't fine. My life had altered. Something had drastically changed in my head. I wasn't normal anymore, that was for sure. Apparently, this was my new life. This was my new normal.

I've always been told, be careful what you wish for. Or in this case, be careful what you pray for. I didn't realize that praying for God to open me up and remove anything that was hindering me, would ever look like this.

I didn't realize that having a revelation that I'm ready to let go of safety and control could actually elevate my blood pressure. I didn't realize that the elevated blood pressure would so quickly be picked up during my vitals check. And I surely didn't know that the fear of something being wrong with my health would trap me in debilitating fear, anxiety and panic attacks for the next whole year.

I had a revelation to let go. I wanted to let go. I really did. But God knew to get me to surrender, He'd have to wrestle me down first. I couldn't see this story so clearly back in 2011, but I see it now.

One of the hardest seasons in my life turned out to be the best thing that ever happened to me. That season of my journey taught me to trust God, stop resisting, and truly let go. It also forced me to be okay with not being okay. I was able to discover what it means to be authentic. My eyes were opened to how unequipped the majority of Believers are when it comes to mental health battles. My eyes also opened to how religion actually contributed to the chains of bondage I found myself trying to break free from.

You see, there are some obstacles in life we cannot overcome just by simply saying we're going to overcome; sometimes we have to go through some serious crap before we overcome. We might have to get sandpapered. We might have to scrape our knees and elbows, and barely survive ... but nonetheless, survive.

I want to share my story of that six-year journey with you, so you'll see both the struggles and the triumphs. I want you to see the failures and the victory. I want you to see that fear does show up and try to stop us, but fear can be engulfed when courage shows up. You have victory over fear.

I want you to know you're not alone as you battle fear or navigate panic. You're not the only one. You're not too far gone. There is hope during your darkest seasons. There is light at the end of the tunnel. As we battle on, we're changed forever because we discover the hidden parts of us that want to be exposed. I wanted to share this journey with you so you can see my struggle with people-pleasing, how the windows of social media destroy us with comparison and a constant desire to be more, do more, show more – so we can feel good about ourselves. I wanted to have a place to share my meltdowns and cussing fits.

I wanted to invite you on my journey as a Christian. I wanted you to see how I'm challenged by church culture verses what the scripture says about Jesus. I want to point out how a skewed perspective actually gave me more anxiety. Church culture caused me to strive harder, perform better, give more and do more. These were cover-ups to keep me from being seen and known. I would do anything to reduce the fear that someone may know me and reject me because they found something wrong with me. Just like the cold that led me to the doctor, led the doctor to find something wrong with me when my blood pressure was elevated.

The truth is, the wrong is there to be found. We can only hide and control for so long before we're found out. It's crucial that we know who we are and live authentically from our truest selves. Hiding who you are leads to anxiety. Even if you don't believe in Jesus, I believe my story will make you feel less alone. I'm not here to convince you to turn to Christ. I just want you to walk through my faith journey with me.

I want to share this journey with you for all the reasons listed above, but most of all, my hope is that as you read my story of how I found my truest self – you'll discover that you're actually on your own journey of finding your truest self. Sometimes we don't recognize our biggest battles are the exact struggle we need to launch us into freedom.

We're in process and becoming more and more who we're meant to be – our truest selves. But we can't get there by standing still, crumbling under fear. We must keep moving, boldly.

~

We are passing through. My friends, we are pressing forward.

ONE

I sat in small group that early Wednesday summer morning, surrounded by women who loved Jesus ... and I felt alone. I listened to their stories of empowerment; how they triumphed through their darkest battles by calling on the name of Jesus Christ. They quoted scriptures and made powerful statements that moved some women to nod their heads in agreement and moved others to tears of hope.

Not me. I sat there numb.

How can I be surrounded by so many godly women and still be so alone? I know everything they're telling me. I know all the truths about Jesus and how our faith expands when we hear the word. For heaven's sake, I used to teach this just a few short months ago when I hosted my own small group.

In a season when I was plagued with fear, I'm not sure how I mustered up enough courage to get myself and my child ready and go to that weekly women's bible study at church. I just knew I had to go. I felt safe there. I felt like maybe this Wednesday will be the day that someone says something that sets me free. Maybe this Wednesday the group of anointed women will lay hands on me and the demon will come out! I figured my freedom was hidden somewhere in that Wednesday gathering.

Instead the group shared remarkable victories, using their beautiful, Christian-culture words. Occasionally a woman would dig in a little deeper, or share a surface-level struggle, but we'd quickly move on.

We went around the circle, answering questions about faith regarding whatever topic we were discussing, when I couldn't hold it in any longer. I interrupted.

"I'm really struggling," I said with tear-filled eyes that were looking past the face of the woman in front of me. "Something is wrong with me. I've prayed. I've repented. I've read the Bible. I've talked with friends. I'm in constant panic. My thoughts are always racing and nothing is helping."

I turned my eyes to look into the faces of the women around me. The group was awkwardly silent. Their eyes moved away from mine. It was as if they were trying to avoid the bomb I just dropped.

"Well ..." a brave voice emerged from the group. "God is good and you may not understand now, but it will all work out. Just keep having faith. This too shall pass."

Then we moved on to the next topic to be discussed. I already felt lonely. Now I felt unseen... and unheard. I felt hopeless. The bible study ended. As I was gathering my purse and bag from my seat, Diana, approached me. I didn't know her very well. We had met a few months earlier, but she had been in my group for the summer. She was kind and gentle.

"April, I know exactly how you feel," she said. "I went through a season with a lot of stress and chaos that challenged me greatly. I would start to panic at random times and feel like I couldn't breathe. I want you to know that You are okay. You're just going through something that you don't understand right now."

She then started to share practical tips for dealing with panic attacks. I was so encouraged by her story and her advice. She wasn't pushing me away with the Christian how-to's. She was giving me practical advice and sharing her real-life, messy story with me.

Diana became such a great friend during this season of my life. She checked in on me regularly to make sure I wasn't becoming too isolated. Instead of rushing me through the process, she met me right where I was, and offered hope in the trenches. Oddly enough, the hope came because she shared her weaknesses with me.

I found that many women did not want to talk about mental health issues. I had no idea that majority of women, Christian or not, were struggling with some sort of mental health disorder. It was a well-kept secret around my tribe.

I was clueless. I thought you could pray away the feelings. After all, I had always been taught that when you call on the name of Jesus, darkness flees.

But I was calling on the name of Jesus. And darkness was not fleeing. Sometimes praying would actually make me feel worse. I assumed it was my fault, that something was wrong with me.

Was I possessed? Was I really a Christian? Had I really confessed all my sins and repented?

In the Christian faith, there is nothing more we can do after we give our lives to Jesus. Yes, we can grow and nurture new disciplines. Yes, we take on a new value and belief system. But there is nothing more we can do to be freer or more saved. It has already been done when Jesus died on the cross.

Still, in my life, I have found that when hard times hit my first reaction is to do something. But doing something wasn't working.

Praying harder, longer, deeper and with a bigger vocabulary wasn't the answer. Lying on my face, getting on my knees, closing my eyes and hiding in my prayer closet wasn't the answer. Joining hands with others in the faith, having them pour oil on me and laying hands on me wasn't the answer. Fasting wasn't the answer, either.

Please don't misunderstand; I wholeheartedly believe in prayer, posture, laying on of hands, fasting and the other spiritual disciplines spoken of in the Bible. Indeed, these things eventually played a huge role in my healing from anxiety and depression. But I had boxed myself in with these answers alone, and when they didn't bring an immediate solution, I was devastated. I started to doubt. I questioned everything I had ever believed.

I was a good girl who loved Jesus and followed the rules. Why the hell was this happening to me? What I didn't know at the time was that I was actually a victim of codependency, people pleasing, shame, guilt and control.

My whole childhood I wanted to belong somewhere. I always felt out of place. My parents were hard workers, but with three kids and limited finances, we didn't have the nicest possessions.

My parents moved from Oklahoma to Tennessee when I was three years old. We lived in a run-down part of the state for a year before my parents moved to a wealthier region of Tennessee. We moved our trailer from Columbia to Franklin and we set up shop.

At four years old, I didn't really care that I lived in a trailer. But once I hit grade school, and realize the other kids lived in brick houses in subdivisions, I found myself aware that I was less than.

I wanted to belong with the cool crowd, so I became a

master impersonator. I could take the cheapest clothing and make it look like good quality. I learned everything I could about their way of life. I mimicked the way their rooms looked. I mimicked the way their closets looked. I begged my mom to buy me a trapper-keeper (remember those?) instead of just the standard, simple, cheaper, hard-plastic binder. I tried to get my mom to buy a minivan that looked like my best friend's minivan.

My mama wasn't havin' it.

I didn't want the life or stuff I had in front of me. I wanted what they had. So, I learned to manipulate the things and people around me to help hide my real life, and project the image that I so desperately wanted.

I succeeded. The problem is that I never felt worthy or good enough. I remember a few years ago having coffee with an old friend, Jessica. I had not seen her in 12 years. Then one day we connected on Facebook, and met up for coffee. We shared about adulthood and marriage, children, homes and all the in between from high school until present time. I told her about my identity journey - how I had always strived to be popular and realized it just wasn't for me.

With a very perplexed looked she started laughing and said, "April, you were popular!"

"Me? No, I wasn't," I said in laughter back at her.

"Yes, you were. You were very popular. My friends and I always saw you as popular."

In that moment I realized, Wow! I had accomplished what I had set out to do. Everyone around me had viewed me as popular ... and yet I never felt popular. I had fooled everyone. I got exactly what I wanted and it still wasn't good enough. I still didn't believe it for myself.

Which showed me the problem wasn't on the outside. The problem was on the inside. The problem was me, or more accurately, the problem was my way of thinking.

There is a reason therapists try to get you to talk about your childhood. There's a lot of jacked-up stuff that got planted in your mind back then. Whether your parents, teachers, friends or perfect strangers meant to jack you up or not, it happened in those childhood years where you're being taught how to be a decent human being.

The problem is, the ones who are teaching you to be a decent human being are jacked-up themselves. They're teaching you their way. They're teaching you from their perspective. You spend your childhood being taught how to be and who to be and then you spend your adulthood trying to undo all that and find out who you really were created to be.

My struggle with anxiety and depression began this *who am I* process for me. It opened the curtains and shined light on shame, doubt, fear, control, people-pleasing, codependency and other things that were hindering me from living free, and preventing me from living wholehearted as the woman I was created to be.

All these rusted traits were linked to fear. Fear was buried in my flower bed.

The flower bed is what my friend Sarah R. referred to when she was describing the unseen parts of our hearts and minds. Sarah was a friend from church, and was the matriarch for this particular season of my life. Outside of the Wednesday women's bible study, my family attended a small group at her house.

I admired Sarah. She was a woman of mystery, but she was sold out for living a life of love. She seemed simple. I wished

I could be more like her. She always had words that were soothing balm during rough patches of my journey.

Sarah had experienced her own battle with anxiety and depression years earlier. She knew what I was going through, even if it looked a little different from her own journey. She understood. One day she was trying to help me look below the surface to get a better idea about what was going on in my life.

"It's kind of like a flower bed," she said. "It can be really pretty to the eye. All the flowers and greenery are growing nice. The soil is dark. Everything looks nurtured and in its place. When in all actuality there are roots from weeds under the soil that are choking out the life of the blooms. These weeds are poison to what's growing above.

Shame, guilt, unforgiveness, are a few roots that may be hiding below the surface. I would encourage you to get on your gardening gear, get your hand shovel, get on the ground and start tending to your flower bed. Find the roots and pull them up. When the weeds appear on the surface you can spend your time continuously chopping them away or you can get down in the dirt, dig deep and create a big ol' mess visually. Find those roots and rip them up. Then you don't have to spend your time keeping up with the weeds; they'll be gone!"

The analogy of a flower bed was perfect. I totally understood what she was talking about. I just didn't know how to start. If I knew what the problem was, I would clean it up. I pondered her words and prayed that God would reveal a starting place for me.

The next day, while driving the car, I pulled up to a red light and looked at my face in the rearview mirror. I didn't recognize myself. I looked different. I didn't look happy.

I used to be so happy.

"I am happy. I've always been happy," I said to myself in the mirror.

As soon as the words came out of my mouth, I thought, But who are you if you're not happy?

I didn't know the answer. If I couldn't hide behind happiness I felt vulnerable. I was too exposed. I was too weak. The broken, shattered me was finally being seen for the first time. It was like a scab over a cut, except my scab wasn't providing a covering for healing - it was just covering up the real wound and preventing healing.

My happiness was gone. My old childhood friends were gone. The church girls didn't get me. I had no appetite, so I couldn't eat to feel comfort. Tony and I were living on one income, so I couldn't spend money for retail therapy. Drinking alcohol just made me more anxious, so that was out. The safety of everything that had once comforted me was nowhere to be found.

And there I was, bowed down in the flower bed of my life. I was scared and alone. I had nowhere to run and nothing to bring me relief. All that was left was surrender ... and surrender felt like lying down to die.

For the first time in my life my flower bed was now destroyed. The flowers were ripped up, the mulch was out of place, piles of dirt surrounded what was once beautiful landscape. And I was down on my knees, covered in sweat, tears and mud, digging to find the roots of deception that were choking out the growth of something beautiful in my life.

Two

Isn't it interesting that this particular place, this bottom of the bottom place is where death occurs and new life is born? I've never seen it happen any other way. As much as I try to resist pain and discomfort, I really have no control over what will inevitably take place.

The more we try to resist, the more we prolong the death experience - which is going to take place anyway. Perhaps it's our need for control; our need to hold fear down, as if we're drowning it out. But we're not drowning it. We're just rolling out the red carpet for fear, placing it on a stage in our lives and making it front and center.

I was terrified of natural death. Talk about no control! Even as a Christian who recognized the glorious mystery of heaven, fear gripped me painfully when it came to the topic of death. The fear of death plagued me when I was struggling with anxiety and depression. I was afraid to drive in the inside lane of the interstate, because I thought I had more control in the outside lane and was closer to the shoulder. Safety was in the outside lane. A semi-truck could kill me in the inside lane, but definitely not in the outside near the shoulder.

There were other ridiculous OCD rituals that helped me function in a false sense of safety. Anything to escape and avoid death. Since I was completely in control of avoiding death (insert sarcasm), death was all around me. It was as if I woke up one morning and realized the world is extremely dangerous. I saw all the opportunities to die and what a miracle it was that most of us even make it through the day alive.

I didn't have to only worry about keeping myself alive, I had a three-year-old daughter and a husband that I needed to keep alive as well. Keeping people alive is far too much a task for a mere human. The pressure and fear were crushing in all around me.

I turned to my faith. As I read the scriptures about death and the glory that awaits a follower of Jesus, I found hope. Reading those passages was like water being poured on hard, dry, cracked dirt. I felt nurtured. It was as if the soil of my heart was being renewed, and a place for new life to emerge was being prepared.

Yet, as much as I felt hopeful, I still lacked understanding. I wanted cold, hard answers that would assure me that everything would be okay.

That evening I listened to a podcast from Bethel Church in Redding, California. Pastor Bill Johnson, the lead pastor, said something that set my soul at ease among my lack of understanding with death. He quoted Philippians 4:7, "and the peace of God, which surpasses all understanding, will guard your hearts and minds through Christ Jesus."

"We all want to experience the peace that passes all understanding," he said. "But our need for control gets in the way." Then he said something which has changed me forever, and I'll quote for the rest of my life.

 "To experience the peace that passes all understanding, you must first give up the need to understand."

He was saying, you have to let go. You have to keep pressing forward not knowing what's on the other side. You have to keep moving. You have to rest in the unknown. You have to be okay with what tomorrow brings.

My fear of death was demolished. Every time I felt the fear of death, and when anxiety would wrap its dirty hands around my neck, instead of letting that fear sit in my mind, I would chase it down to the point of death.

What's the worst that will happen? I grocery shop, my heart starts beating fast. I can either keep grocery shopping, pressing forward through the uncomfortable feelings, or the worst-case scenario is I die.

Jogging in the park was terrifying to me, because anytime you exercise your heart rate goes up and you experience all kinds of discomfort in your body. For you normal folks, that's not much of a problem. You don't feel these things. But for those of us who have had the curtain opened in our minds, we feel the discomfort. We feel everything from our heart beating uncontrollably, to our toes tingling.

As I jogged, overwhelming thoughts about how I was going to die would flood my mind. I had to chase that fear down to the point of death.

What's the worst that could happen? Well, I'm jogging, which is good for me. I've been told by multiple medical professionals that I'm 'fine'. If I die jogging then at least I was doing something good for my health when I died.

I stopped caring about dying. I mean, sometimes I cared and felt afraid, but I didn't let it stop me from doing the things I needed to do. I'd be the worst kidnapping victim. I can't handle my head being messed with so if someone was threatening to kill me over and over again, I'd either fight them to make them kill me, or I'd run away and be so defiant that they'd have to kill me. "Pull the trigger already. I don't have time for the drama. Just take me out!"

That's pretty much how the fear of death went down in my life. I don't have time for your drama. If you're going to kill me, kill me - but until then, I have errands to run and business to take care of. I gave an open invitation to death. I wasn't going to fear it any longer. I wasn't going to let it dictate my life for another moment.

The peace that passes understanding did fill my mind, but only when I gave up the need to understand. I did not need to spend my time and energy avoiding death any longer.

One thing we all have in common is death. We're not getting out of here alive - not one of us. I believe we die tiny deaths all throughout our lives. We die to ourselves. Our old ideas of who we are or who everyone wants us to be - they either die of terminal illness or we murder them.

One way or another death occurs. You can't resist death. You can make wiser choices and decisions to prolong life, but death ultimately swallows us up. I believe this is true not only for natural life, but for the process of our lives.

Years after my battle with anxiety and depression, I was in a healthy place mentally, as far as my actions not being dictated by paralyzing fear. But I was dying to some old ideals. My husband had left his corporate IT job and was stepping out on faith to start his own IT business. No one in our family has ever started their own business. I mean, no one has even graduated from college, let alone start a business.

The idea of starting a business and actually making money was terrifying. We were blocked in our minds.

My friend, Melissa, owns her own business with her

husband. They have been entrepreneurs for years. I love being around her and hearing their new, exciting ideas and their adventures with business.

To her, the idea of owning a business is a real thing, because she lives it out every day. To me and Tony, the idea of owning a business seemed so far off. We would have to jump trenches, navigate valleys and climb mountains to get to the destiny of being business owners.

I kept seeing a picture of a brick wall in my mind when it came to starting the business. All the fear surrounding questions like:

How do we create a legal business?

Are we really going to empty our savings to start this business when we're already on one income?

Who's going to buy these services, anyway? What about health insurance?

Businesses get sued, you know. What if we get sued?

It was paralyzing!

One day I talked to my friend, Melissa about the brick wall. I said, "I see this brick wall when it comes to this business. It's like we're standing there and we can hear people on the other side. There is activity over there. There's life and abundance. We know it's there, but we don't know how to get there.

So, we take this chisel and we pound at these bricks day after day until we'll eventually get through to the other side."

She looked at me with her Oh-April-why-do-you-over-complicate-everything type of smile (which I'm used to with her) and said, "Or, you could just climb over."

Drop. The. Mic.

I had never considered climbing over the brick wall. I had never considered the fact that my husband and I were worthy of being entrepreneurs, successful business owners. I had never considered that the brick wall was an obstacle that most people who are stepping out on faith and risk, must navigate - over, under, around or through. It wasn't just a special brick wall, placed there for only me and Tony.

As Tony and I navigated the season of starting a business, we thought we were losing our godforsaken minds. Trust me; starting a business is not for the faint of heart. It's extremely challenging.

We did start the business and it did have lots of success, but it was only for a short season. I don't think that business was ever meant to be a multi-million-dollar company. I believe that business was another opportunity to die a tiny death.

Everything I had ever known about myself was pretty much already gone from previous tiny deaths, but it was something about this season that I felt April, the April I had always known since childhood, was dying. I had come to a place in my life where I was tired of all my dreams falling apart.

Right after my fight with anxiety in 2011, I started a ministry called Healed Whole New, for Christian women who battle with anxiety and depression. I poured my heart and soul into that ministry. So much time over a three-year span went to that ministry.

We helped women all over the world understand that they were not alone in their battles. We brought awareness to the silent bully of mental health battles in Christian circles. I just knew this ministry would make it 'big time,' and I could quit my corporate job at last and work in ministry full time.

Not so much.

During intense prayer one evening, I felt God ask me to give up the ministry.

"But I have worked so hard, Lord," I exclaimed at Him.

As that final word left my mouth, I fell to my knees and wept. Realization set in. This was not His ministry. This was *my* ministry. This was *my* opportunity to be seen - in the Name of Jesus, of course (insert sarcasm).

I immediately surrendered the ministry and returned to a corporate job in Human Resources, which is what my background had been for years.

There were so many other dreams and visions that fell apart. There were so many job losses in my and Tony's marriage history together. At the beginning of our marriage we lost a home, two years after we bought it. We had cars taken from us due to the job losses. We had both lost friends, either because they walked away from us or because we had to walk away from them. I had done everything as right as I knew how, and we still weren't getting ahead.

I stood in my bedroom putting folded clothes into the dresser drawers. I had felt a deep sadness for days. I hadn't experienced deep grief in my life from losing a loved one, but I imagined this feeling was that type of grief. I didn't know what to do with it, and I couldn't escape it. What a horrible internal feeling.

I looked into the mirror and saw Tony walking down the hallway toward me. With tears streaming down my face, I buried myself into his chest. We stood there in the silence. Only my tearful breathing broke the quiet of the room.

"I feel like I'm dying," I said through tears. "April, the only person I've ever known; it's like she's dying. If I let her go, she's gone. It feels like I'm losing my best friend and I'll be all alone. I've let go of so much already."

Tony rubbed my back. He's the most patient person I know

and tends to take time to think before he speaks. Which means he usually doesn't get a word in when I'm around.

I continued, "I'm grieving the death of myself and all my dreams, of my life planned out the way I wanted it to be. She's dying, Tony. That's why I'm so angry lately, and so emotional."

Tony responded, "You've just got to let go. Don't resist. Just let go."

A couple of days later I was at my chiropractor's office. I had been battling the aftershocks of bronchitis for a while and figured an adjustment and some acupuncture would help. Dr. Dearing had worked on me for quite some time that October with this particular bout of bronchitis. As he was inserting the acupuncture needles, he said, "In ancient Chinese medicine, irritation in the lungs represents metal, which represents grief. Are you holding on to the loss of a loved one or something?"

I was face down on the table with my eyes closed until he made that statement. My eyes flew open wide. I looked down at that floor through the head rest and said, "Something like that."

"I'm going to leave you in here for about 20 minutes with the needles, and I want you to focus on releasing that grief. Let it run through you, press through it and then let it go," he said as he left the room, closing the door behind him.

I lay there, face-down, with tears streaming. It was a gut-wrenching cry that came from somewhere deep down. I knew it was time to press forward, but the only way to move on was to let go. I had to let her die.

And so, I did. There in that chiropractic office with acupuncture needles in my back, with the ugly-cry activated, moving through the breathtaking fear of what if, I surrendered to the tiny death - and let April, as I knew her, go.

Those tiny deaths that meet us throughout this journey of life are inevitable. You can't negotiate with them; just like you can't negotiate with natural death. They will come for you.

The only difference with the tiny deaths is that you can surrender, lay down and die, which ultimately results in new life. Or you can decline the death. The problem is, if you decline and refuse to surrender, you don't die - but the death remains around you. You carry it with you throughout the rest of your natural life. So, each time a tiny death shows up and you don't die, it attaches itself to you along with the other tiny deaths you didn't accept.

We all know the people who walk around with death attached to them. They are bitter, and angry at people and life. They harvest unforgiveness. They stopped growing years ago. They are not open for change. They are usually the most judgmental, critical, gossipy, negative, victimized people you know. Death offered itself to them, and they declined.

You see, this type of death, a surrendered death, is the only way new life emerges from the ashes. These tiny deaths show us where we've gone wrong. They show us how far off-course we are. The life that emerges puts us back on track. It peels back another layer of who we were created to be. It launches us into wholeness and into our very purpose for living on this earth.

Whether your greatest fear is natural death or the tiny deaths I speak of here, you're not alone. We fear all the above at one point or another because it requires change. I'm sure you'd agree our greatest strength is not change. But to press forward we must let go. We must allow change. We have to die. We can't stop it anyway. We can prolong the process, we can collect the tiny deaths and become nasty and bitter. Or we can let go, surrender and die to have new life emerge.

THREE

After giving up Healed Whole New, the ministry I had worked diligently on for three years, I was offered a position in Human Resources with a company that offers addiction and mental health treatment to people who are battling with substance abuse. I had never been so close to what we call the 'underbelly' of the world.

I had been attending churches in the county for 10 years at this point and found myself pissed off at the church. I was never told about the underbelly. No one talked about it or really ministered to it.

Why? Why weren't we having these conversations at church or in our small groups? I had been extremely involved in church groups throughout those 10 years, and never was a part of a conversation about people struggling with mental health battles or substance abuse.

When I took the HR job, especially since I was coming out of ministry and had just surrendered my plan for God's plan, I just knew this would be my mission ground. I was going to go to this company and help save the souls of many. A lot of our employees were in recovery themselves and I just couldn't wait to share the Good News with them - discreetly, of course. I mean, I was in Human Resources.

Working with these folks was transformative, but after a year and a half in HR, I felt I needed a change. I wanted to be in the trenches. I could not be that close to where help was needed and not be a part of it. I left my career, 13 years in HR and took on a whole new role - Admissions Manager at the same company.

Moving onto the Admissions Team, managing a team of 10 Treatment Specialists, definitely turned my world upside down. I had never met such real people in my life. The people I worked with had gone through life or death ... literally. Their stories were overwhelming. To look into the eyes of someone, like my friend Kiersten, whose husband overdosed and died in his sleep right beside her, will take your breath away. The fact that she gets up every morning, stays sober and faces the challenges of the day with courage is admirable. Or Amy, who just celebrated eight years clean from alcohol. You would never imagine what she has overcome when you see her big, bright smile. Or Cory, who lives life with zeal after literally being brought back to life from a heroin overdose.

When I first started with the company I thought I would show up and change the hearts of the people around me. Instead the people around me changed my heart. In fact, they pretty much ripped my heart out. You see, I had always stood on the sidelines of life and preached from the outside.

Addiction and mental health disorders scared me. I thought if I got too close, what they had might rub off on me. I kept my preaching shoes polished and clothes pressed. But when I started working in behavioral health, I noticed my shoes started to get dirty and my clothes started to get wrinkled. I was sitting among the people instead of preaching from the outside.

Working on the HR side of the company and the Admissions side brought incredible growth to my life. During the HR season, my boss was a follower of Christ and a PhD psychologist. Dr. Brooks taught me so much about Human Resources, conflict resolution, employee development and management on the professional front. But he also taught me about being open-minded, the heart of Jesus, personal development, and he straight-up counseled me as my world was being turned upside-down, because I was in shock from experiencing the underbelly of the world.

In 2011, during my season of anxiety, my friend Sarah had recommended I go to counseling or therapy. I couldn't afford it at the time. I remember trying to go through the church. They charged on a sliding scale, but their sliding scale was still too steep for my family at the time, so I never got counseling. I trudged through the anxiety and depression and overcame. Since I had overcome, I started a ministry to tell everyone how I had overcome and you could too!

The problem is - I had never overcome. I just learned to press forward with the anxiety. It wasn't stopping me from living life, but I was definitely still living with anxiety. I did not know this until I met Dr. Brooks.

I found it humorous during this season in behavioral health because God was ripping my heart out (for my own good) and tearing down walls I had built up with judgment and criticism toward anyone who wasn't like me or anyone who didn't believe what I believed. The humor came when I realized how often I had called people crazy and made comments about how others needed counseling in the past. My own critical heart was quick to toss a judgment onto someone else because of my lack of understanding.

I remember laughing in my office one day and saying aloud, "Wow, God. Really? I was always calling people crazy and yet I'm so flippin' crazy you have paired me with a PhD Psychologist to work with, day in and day out, professionally and personally. That's how crazy You think I am?"

The more I saw how messed up I was and how much help I needed, it made me laugh a lot. I may not have gotten therapy in 2011, but I surely got some help getting unstuck in 2015 when I worked in HR in the behavioral health field alongside Dr. Brooks.

Shortly after I started the job, Dr. Brooks and I took a road trip from Tennessee to Mississippi. This car ride is etched into my memory forever, in part because we ate donuts from a gas station that tried to kill us! These exploding donuts looked delicious in the packaging, and we both had a sweet tooth, but once we popped a mini-donut in our mouths it exploded into a dry pastry that literally sucked every ounce of moisture out of our mouths. We laughed so hard. I cried from laughing at Dr. Brook's reaction to the donuts.

I have such great memories from that road trip. Just the excitement of meeting our wonderful staff at the substance abuse treatment facility for the first time, listening to worship songs in the car, talking about the company and the vision for the future, sharing about our families.

But the most memorable and life changing part of this particular trip was when I shared a weakness with Dr. Brooks about the anxiety I had right there, real time, while I was riding beside him. Sharing weakness was new to me, but I felt safe from judgment with him, and I wanted help.

"I feel afraid. I feel scared that we're leaving Tennessee and that something bad could happen. I know that's silly and nothing is going to happen - and even if it does there's nothing I can do about it. I'll press through this fear and go to Mississippi and function as the HR Manager, but I feel locked up and afraid right this very moment," I said to Dr. Brooks as he was looking straight out the windshield, keeping his eyes on the road.

He listened intently and I continued, "I'll fight this anxiety and I'll win." I felt powerful with my response. I had learned how to put anxiety in its place when it tried to mess with me. This is what I did all through the season in 2011 when I was plagued with anxiety. It's what I taught women to do through Healed Whole New.

Fight. Battle. Win. Repeat.

I felt powerful with my quick cover up response to my confession of weakness, but what I think Dr. Brooks heard was a cry for help. I think he saw a young woman with an image of courage to battle anxiety, but he saw through the facade. I think he could see I had gotten so far out, I couldn't turn back and say, "I'm scared. Am I doing this right? Am I really healed? Do I have a mental health issue? Do I need medication? Is there something wrong with me?"

And honestly, if he was thinking all those things about me, he was right. The last thing I wanted to hear was that something was wrong with me and he could clearly see it. I mean, that is what started all this crap back in 2011. I was told something was wrong with me. When the doctor saw that my blood pressure was high, she saw something wrong with me. I don't think that trip to the doctor that pushed me over the cliff of anxiety was ever about a health scare - it was about the fact that someone identified something wrong with me. The shame that consumed my heart and mind was front and center. I'm not good enough. I'm not enough. I'm broken. Something is wrong with me. I was an impersonator remember? I had learned to fit in, to belong, to mimic what those around me saw as acceptable.

I knew Dr. Brooks could see though. Except he didn't see something wrong with me. He simply saw a girl stuck on an island of false healing, pleading for a life raft, for someone to come get her. Shoot, I didn't even see it. His words that day in the car literally set me free.

After listening to me try to convince him and ultimately try to convince myself about what a great warrior I was when it came to overcoming anxiety, Dr. Brooks started to talk about simple truths regarding Jesus. His words comforted my aching soul. It was as if he stripped away all the confusion and shot directly into my heart the simple words that would loosen the grip of the chains I had carried around for four years.

I'm a doer. It's what I do. I don't sit in silence or nothingness. I do. So, it wasn't shocking that when Dr. Brooks finished sharing his lovely words about Jesus, my immediate reaction was to do something.

I said, "Thank you for sharing all that, Dr. Brooks. You're right. I need to continue to speak truth over the battle and fight anxiety with truth."

He said, "Your battle is not against anxiety. Your battle is against the resistance to go to Jesus when anxiety comes."

Those words were the key that unlocked anxiety's death grip on me. After Dr. Brooks said this to me I could literally feel the grip of what felt like hands around my neck, release and go away. I immediately took a deep breath. It was as if I was breathing for the first time. That grip of fear that constantly harassed me; the fear I had learned to press through and carry on living my life - for the first time in four years was gone.

The battle could not be won in my doing. It was won in the waiting - in the in-between. It wasn't during one of my best performances or powerful teachings about Jesus. The battle was won simply during a car ride for a business trip when I was completely vulnerable, completely seen, and listening instead of talking; while I was learning, instead of teaching.

The battle was won in my surrender. Being broken is what healed me. Perfect Strength was found in my weakest place - being seen.

FOUR

One day, on the way home from work, Sway, my baby boy, was in the back seat playing with his small Matchbox cars as we were headed to our side of town to pick up Trinity from her after school program. I could see the traffic building up ahead; the stream of red brake lights as far as I could see. I felt the panic inside of me and tried to get over two lanes of traffic to get off at the exit prior to the exit that takes us home.

It was too late. I was stuck.

If only I had merged over sooner, I wouldn't be stuck sitting in traffic. As we came to a complete stop I felt myself getting extremely overwhelmed. It was hard to catch my breath and I felt panic sinking in.

Stop! I thought. This is stupid. Calm down. You're just in traffic. It's not the end of the world. I still felt on edge and wanted to cry. Ugh! I just have to sit in it.

I thought about how often I hate 'sitting in it.' I would rather take a detour, miles out of the way, just as long as I can keep moving. I felt a revelation in my spirit. I never sit in it. In anything. I keep moving and doing and going and striving, just so I won't have to sit in it. I stay busy. I detour to keep moving instead of sitting still and letting the moment be the moment – good or bad, whatever.

As I sat there in the traffic I yelled out to myself, "Suck it up!"

"Suck it up, Mommy," came from a little voice from the back seat. Sway was smiling from ear to ear. "Suck it up, Mommy," he said again. I looked at him in the rearview mirror, then turned my head around and laughed at him. "Yeah. Suck it up Mommy," I said to him about myself.

We both yelled, "Suck it up, Mommy!" a few more times and laughed at each other. I forgot about the panic. The fear had lifted. It had been swallowed up in a moment shared between me and my son. The traffic started to move and we carried on with our evening routine.

Later that evening, I sat on the patio under the streamed lights that a friend had hung for me and Tony earlier that month and stared at the stars. I took a deep breath in and reflected on the traffic drama from earlier. Where did such fear come from? Why was I so overwhelmed? The issue was way deeper than a traffic jam. What was up with me not sitting in it?

Why am I so busy and always moving, going, creating, doing?

Sitting there with those thoughts I realized that sitting in it means no control. I couldn't control that traffic. If we sat there all night, I was stuck. There was nothing I could do to make us move again.

Why is that such a big deal? Where am I rushing to? Why am I in such a hurry? Why am I anxious when I can't move forward? As I pondered these questions, I thought back to the year 2011 when I suffered from paralyzing anxiety and depression that nearly took my life. I battled so hard during that season. It was dark and lonely. No one understood. I was ill. My thoughts were loud, catastrophic and exhausting all day and all night long.

One night, during that season, while my family was sleeping, I fell on my face and cried out to God to help me. I was tired of running and trying to fix it myself. The scripture came to mind where Jesus was asking his disciples - after the crowd stopped following him because his message was too hard - if they were going to leave him too. I could hear Peter through my sobbing on the floor. "Simon Peter answered him, "Lord, to whom shall we go? You have the words of eternal life." (John 6:68)

I was resolved at that point that I wasn't turning my back on Jesus, no matter how bad it hurt. I had to trust him over my feelings. There was nowhere else to turn. Only Jesus had the words of eternal life. I was not giving up. I promised myself I would keep pressing forward. Even on my worst days, I made a choice to keep moving.

I had come so far from 2011 but sitting in traffic earlier that evening really covered me with anxiety that reminded me of my struggle in 2011. Thinking of 2011 and anxiety made me reflect deeper about anxiety. To me, 2011 was my first experience with anxiety, or so I thought. It was so foreign to me. I think that's why it scared me so much, because it was not familiar. I had never experienced anything like it before. Over the years I have been able to see that anxiety manifests in different ways. It's not always in your face, catastrophic, take you down and try to kill you. Sometimes it's subtle.

I slid down in my chair and exhaled. Looking up at the lights on my patio again, I started to think about when I was a kid. The breeze whipped around the patio and blew my hair back. I closed my eyes and breathed in the smell of fresh air as I listened to the crickets and the orchestra of other sounds coming from the trees and bushes not far from where I was relaxing. Clinching my eyes as if it would help me remember better, I pictured myself as a five-year-old girl running around the yard at my house on a summer day. I pictured myself at school and with my friends. I remembered Christmas Eve and the warmth of our home, the fun I had with my brothers. I was the only girl between two brothers and life was always interesting with them around.

I smiled thinking about them.

I thought about Christmas Eve night at our house, well actually it was Christmas Eve Eve. Our family tradition was to open gifts on Christmas Eve and open Santa gifts on Christmas day. It was awesome! So, on Christmas Eve Eve I would be overly excited about the next morning.

My brothers would be excited too, but when it was time for bed they would quickly fall asleep. The sooner you fell asleep the sooner morning would come. Not for me, though. I wanted to go to sleep so bad, but I just couldn't. I would lie there with my eyes wide open, feeling completely alert and awake. Then I would close my eyes and lie still for hours but I wouldn't get tired. I'd toss and turn and switch my pillow around. I'd lie at the foot of my bed to change directions and maybe get more comfortable.

I was restless. Sometimes I would finally fall asleep a couple of hours before dawn, and sometimes I would just stay up all night and watch TV. I had so much adrenaline the next morning that I wouldn't feel tired. I had energy all day, but internally felt fatigued and would eventually crash later that evening.

The memory quickly faded as I sat up from my chair on the patio with my eyes wide open. Anxiety? That was anxiety! I then thought about when I would perform in talent shows or anything that I did in front of people. I loved the crowd, loved performing, loved playing sports. I remember being extremely excited and feeling like I couldn't calm down. I would feel excited and sick. I'd lose my appetite and get a burst of adrenaline. I always knew I was an extrovert but when I got around people I would become overly talkative and impulsive. I'd say stupid things and then be annoyed with myself for saying the things I said.

I hated surprises when I knew there was a surprise but didn't know the details. I would feel nervous if between classes in school, a friend told me they needed to tell me something but it would have to wait. Waiting felt painful. I wanted to know everything now.

I sat there on my patio in complete disarray as the memories flooded my mind. It was as if I had just discovered something new about someone I'd known my whole life. I guess I had just made an amazing discovery.

Anxiety had been subtle in my life as far back as I can remember. So many of my childhood memories reflect anxiety. It had always been there, lurking. No wonder at 26 years old it locked its grip around me. It was always weaving a web of deception in my life. It just waited for the perfect opportunity to take me captive.

This explains why I hate sitting in it. Sitting in traffic made me slow down. Sitting through a year of anxiety made me slow down. That year was a year of battle and reflection. Old lies were being uprooted and a new foundation was being laid in my life.

2011 was the worst year of my life, and yet the best year. I learned to depend on God through a true life or death season. I learned that it was extremely uncomfortable to trust God when my life felt out of control and my feelings were numbing me.

It was hard to trust when I didn't see a solution and nothing was saving me or fixing my situation fast enough.

Underneath the pain I held on to hope. I had to hold on, endure and press forward.

I'm convinced that to have breakthrough we have to 'go through.' We can't grow and change without going through something. When I think about all the challenges I have overcome in my life that made me stronger and wiser, it was due to 'go through.' Overcoming anxiety and depression required 'go through.' I had to face each day. I had to get up and push through when I wanted to lie down and die.

Going through that season is what caused a breakthrough and ultimately set me free from the bondage of general anxiety disorder. I was forced to sit in it when that awful season showed up in 2011. Sitting in it isn't one of my strengths at all.

I believe sometimes we are forced into a 'go through' season and sometimes we get to choose if we want to enter into a 'go through' season. Either way, we must trust the process and if you're a believer, we must trust God with the process. Even when it hurts and we don't understand, I believe God is good and will complete the work He has started.

Sitting in traffic that day and the panic that emerged led me to reflect and discover the root of anxiety in my life. Anxiety is a byproduct of fear. Perfect love casts out fear. Why was I not grasping God's perfect love in my life? Standing up on the patio, I looked up at the stars and marveled at them. Perplexed about my discoveries that night, I sighed.

"Why am I not grasping your perfect love?" I said aloud to God. "Why am I holding on to fear? I'm missing something obviously."

I didn't feel defeated, just humbled. I knew I didn't have

the answers for myself. Anxiety was still present in my life, which meant fear was present, which meant I wasn't grasping perfect love. I would have to sit in it and go through a little longer for breakthrough to take place.

Fear was losing its footing in my life. The conversation with Dr. Brooks on the way to Mississippi removed the debilitating fear that had kept a hold on me, but it refused to let me go. I had had enough. That night on the patio I realized my whole view about fear had changed. You don't overcome fear; you press forward when fear comes.

Anytime you enter new territory, fear is going to show up. The unknown will always bring fear but we don't have to ball up in a corner and hide away. No! You face fear. You stand tall and courageous even when your legs are shaking. You hold your ground and endure. Fear will always lose its grip when you take a stand. It will lose its scare tactics when you resolve to keep going. Even if that means sitting in discomfort, or standing alone. Even if that means letting yourself be undone and allowing your true self to shine through. Sometimes you just have to suck it up, stop resisting the fear and be brave enough to sit still and endure. Even in the stillness you are pressing forward.

FIVE

I parked the car under the drive-up awning at Sway's daycare that Friday afternoon.

I looked directly straight ahead through the windshield and could see the kids playing on the playground in the distance on that warm, fall evening. The trees had started to change colors and the dead leaves were tossed in disarray all throughout the daycare property. The sun reflected back from the metal linked fence that was just a short distance away. Kids were running carefree. I could hear their laughter, even with the windows rolled up.

There's nothing like the energy of three-year-olds on a playground. I watched my sweet Sway climb onto the picnic table and jump off repeatedly. He had the carefree smile that only children wear. Sway didn't mind that the other children were playing tag, sliding down slides, working their way across monkey bars or swinging. He had created his own fun with the picnic table. I admired his courage to do his own thing. He didn't care about belonging, or fitting in, or doing what the cool kids were doing.

I smiled at my boy, then dropped my face in my hands and cried.

"Weak!" I said to myself. "What is wrong with me?"

I hated that my son was having a hard time in his new classroom at daycare. A few weeks earlier Tony and I were getting calls and emails that Sway was showing aggression in the classroom and would not be able to continue attending the preschool if his behavior didn't change quickly. I didn't know of the behavior the teachers were referring to until I saw it for myself as I was standing with a teacher during morning drop off a couple of weeks before. After a child snatched something out of Sway's hand, my son, my precious baby boy, picked up a hand full of hard wood blocks and threw them at all the children sitting in the circle.

"Sway!" I yelled, interrupting Mrs. Kate, Sway's teacher, in mid-sentence. Sway made eye contact with me. His eyes looked sad and guilty. He must have forgotten I was in the classroom and upon making eye contact with mommy, he knew he was not only wrong, but caught.

His sad eyes quickly turned to angry eyes. It was as if he didn't care that he hurt others or that his mother had seen him in action.

"Sorry, Kate," I said, as I rushed quickly over to Sway. I knelt down to get on an eye level with him. Rubbing his arms downward and gripping him firmly, I caught his eye and said, "Buddy. No. We can't hurt our friends. You know we don't throw."

Sway pulled against my grip as if he were uncomfortable and wiggled himself back from me. I pulled him back toward me, hugged him, held him close and kissed his forehead. "Be nice to your friends. No throwing," I said.

As he ran off to play, I stood up, made eye contact with Mrs. Kate and did the walk of shame back over toward her.

"He's been throwing, hitting, spitting, scratching, not

listening for quite some time now," Mrs. Kate said.

My eyes moved from Mrs. Kate's and back over to Sway, who was now playing calmly with a train by himself. I didn't want to hear anymore. I wanted to run and pick Sway up, toss him over my shoulder, make a run for it and never return.

They didn't understand him. They weren't trying to get on his level and truly find out what was going on with him. They were judging him, and because he was not the same as others or as easy to handle as the other children, they were picking out pesky things that all kids do and making it a big deal.

He's three. Gosh! What do you expect from a three-year-old? What is this – a boot camp? I need to save him. He can't stay here. I looked back over at Mrs. Kate. Her lips were still moving.

I wasn't listening though. It was as if time had slowed down and the atmosphere around me grew silent. Mrs. Kate looked concerned. We stood there in silence, watching Sway for a moment.

"I'm sorry," I said. "I'm not sure what's going on. I haven't seen any of this behavior at home."

I had to get to work, so I tried to smooth things over the best I could. "Maybe it's because his daddy is out of town. Tony will be back in a few days and hopefully this behavior will stop."

"Maybe. Hopefully," Mrs. Kate said.

I waved goodbye to Sway, thanked Mrs. Kate and wished her a good day and left the room. Walking back to my car, my mind was flooded with thoughts.

He's regressing. He's been out of therapy for a couple of months and it was too soon. If he gets kicked out of daycare where is he going to go? He's verbally delayed and I don't trust other daycares.

This school and their staff have been so good to him. I'm going to have to quit my job.

Tears filled my eyes. I felt helpless.

Sway is my baby boy. He was born in 2013. As much as he's a sweet and funny little addition to our family, he's definitely given us a run for our money. Sway was born with torticollis. Torticollis is a muscle spasm in the neck. It's fixable, but unfortunately for Sway, the pediatrician didn't notice he had torticollis until he was about three months old. He missed out on three months of important development.

Upon this discovery, we took Sway to our chiropractor and within a couple of weeks the spasm was worked out and Sway had rotation in his neck. We were thrilled with the results but those three months gave our boy some serious oral motor setbacks that we would later discover throughout the end of his first year of life.

At each well-child visit with Sway's pediatrician, we saw that Sway was delayed in certain areas of development. He didn't want to eat food or touch certain textures. He had some motor function delay and speech delays as well. He was also diagnosed with Sensory Processing Disorder. Sway is a sensory seeker, meaning he really enjoys jumping, wrestling, being thrust upward, like on a swing or when his dad would toss him up into the air.

Sounds like a boy, right?

He was uncomfortable around loud noises such as vacuums, blenders, or sirens. Those sounds can be uncomfortable for typical folks, but for Sway it's piercing and painful.

I could see that Sway was unique, but I didn't see anything wrong with him. He was different and that was okay.

Because Sway was delayed in so many areas, the pediatrician

recommended we get Sway into therapy - sooner rather than later.

We did.

The state of Tennessee offered free therapy services for children under three years old through a service called Tennessee Early Intervention System (TEIS). We are so grateful for TEIS. The team loved our boy well and believed in him every step of the way. Then Sway turned three. The services immediately ended. A month later at Sway's preschool, all the children moved up to the next class.

Sway was now tolerating certain foods and communicating so much better than before, but he was still just a little behind his classmates. His speech delay was causing him frustration. The frustration was manifesting into aggression.

Sway couldn't verbally communicate what he wanted, or what was bothering him, or speak up for himself, and this was causing him to show hostility. I understood exactly what Sway was going through. I had felt the same way for quite some time. Not necessarily with a speech delay, but just so much pinned up in my heart and mind that I couldn't express.

I tried to share my own story with people around me, but they looked at me with confused eyes. I grew more and more frustrated each time I tried to explain myself. I was looking for help, or relief, or someone to just hug me, but they didn't understand.

Sway threw blocks. I sat in the parking lot and cried. We had our own way of expressing our frustration.

~

Sitting there in my car, watching my boy play alone, jumping off the picnic table without a care in the world, I wiped my tears and tried to fix my makeup. I didn't want anyone to see me crying or ask what was wrong with me. I needed to gather myself and be strong. I was always strong.

I have spent many years being a strong Christian; whatever that means. I have encouraged and led women who were struggling in their faith. I have cheered people on who wanted to quit. I was an advocate for overcoming mental battles, especially anxiety and depression. I was a ministry leader, a voice in social media that spoke up for the underdog and stood firm on the Word of God, teaching women's Bible studies, leading prayer groups and worship nights. There was no time to cry or feel small.

As I touched up the makeup under my eyes, the email alert sounded on my phone. It was from Diana Kerr, a Christian life coach I had started following on social media earlier in the year. I had signed up for her newsletter, and she had sent a message to her followers titled, "You're at war. "The title caught my attention. I certainly felt like I was at war inside myself. I opened the email immediately. The message said:

"Hey, April!

I know we're normally all like "Wheeee! It's the weekend!" on Fridays, but I've got something serious for you to consider before you check out for the weekend.

You're at war.

With yourself, with Satan, and with the world. The Bible says so!

I'm especially concerned about that sneaky Satan, that truth-twisting lion who's out to drag you down and ruin your life and salvation.

Satan loves it when you're distracted, overwhelmed, impatient, emotionally unstable, etc.

It's easier for him to get his way under those circumstances. Are you okay with that?

I'm not!!!   •

I know, this is dramatic and serious, but you know it's true. And here's why I bring this up:

When I remember this truth, it makes me pretty fired up and ready to do anything I can through God's power to make sure Satan has as few victories as possible in my life.

(Thankfully, the ultimate victory is the Lord's, and therefore ours, too, but that doesn't mean Satan doesn't get the best of us from day to day.)

As much as I can, I draw on the Spirit's power within me to resist building a life that's full of meaningless distractions, that consists of stuff that doesn't really matter, that measures up to the world's standards instead of God's.

Does this fire you up too, friend?

The good news is, you are not helpless in this war!

Being close to the Lord and surrounding yourself with the right people and the right content (like being on this email list!) are a great step in the right direction.

Make it a great week of battle in the Lord!"

I started to cry again and wrote Diana a quick note back:

"Right on time. Sitting in a parking lot about to pick my three-year-old up from daycare. Just sitting here crying. Frustrated.

My son is stuck in an awkward place in the world. He's not necessarily "special needs" but he has had some early developmental delays - so he's not where he's "supposed to be" at three years old.

He's having challenges in daycare where he's showing aggressive behavior because his speech is delayed and he's frustrated, so he's throwing, hitting, spitting and throwing fits.

The school is saying he can't continue going here (understandably) if the behavior doesn't change. My husband and I both work full time and are not in a place financially to quit.

So- all that to say- I've given a lot of time and energy to worldly worries lately.

I'm a speaker and writer who encourages other women to hold on and press forward and give it to God- and here I am... losing it in a parking lot.

Your message was timely and lovely and the truth that I needed to get out of this car with my head held high, knowing God sees this. He's got it. He never lost control of it.

Thank you for doing what you do. Blessings my friend!"

Diana's message reminded me that I wasn't alone and I wasn't experiencing anything new that someone else hasn't already experienced. Later that night as I was tidying up my bedroom I received a response from Diana. It leveled me.

"Oh, April. I can imagine that would be stressful and frustrating and scary and hard. I am so, so thankful you have God in your corner in all of this. He is so with you, and not just with you, but he's in control! He's got this in his hands. I know that's harder to truly absorb than it is to just believe it intellectually, but if you're struggling with that tell him that and ask him to make it feel real to you. Love you tons! And by the way, it's okay to be an encourager who cries in parking lots. That makes you more equipped to do what you do. :) Diana"

"It's okay to be an encourager who cries in parking lots. That makes you more equipped to do what you do." Do you know what this said to me? It said, it's okay to be human. It's okay to be alive. It's okay to experience emotion and feelings that aren't always pretty. It's okay to struggle and fall short and be messy sometimes. I was reminded in that moment that God's power was made perfect in my weakness. It now makes me giggle to think that God would use our strengths to bring him glory. No, our strengths bring us glory. It is through our weaknesses that God's power and glory shines through.

I sat on the bed, in the silence of the night. The kids were in bed and Tony was watching TV in the living room. I could feel something moving in my soul. I guess it can sound kind of silly to the outside world but I could feel myself changing ... again.

Years of following Jesus and I realized I was doing it all wrong. I felt trapped. I had built a pretty Christian outer shell and was great at performing and seeking Jesus with an audience and a platform. But I was left empty at the end of the day. I felt like I was wearing an itchy coat that was way too big for me. It didn't fit.

Years of watching great Christian leaders and I had perfected my craft. I had learned to look just like everyone else around me. I had learned to speak that Christianese language that everyone else spoke. I had built a facade of community; and I was lonely. After spending my whole life people pleasing and mimicking what was 'cool' around me, I hit a wall.

As I sat there on the bed, my mind wandered to earlier that evening, watching Sway jump off the picnic table. I admired Sway. Sway didn't care what the world around him was doing. Sway didn't care about the norm. Sway didn't care about what others thought or what the other kids were doing on the playground. Sway was doing what he wanted to do. He made a game out of climbing the picnic table and then jumping off. He was open to others joining him, but if they didn't want to join, he didn't let them stop him.

I wanted that for my own life. The world may think a kid playing alone is strange or isolated or wrong. But I don't see anything wrong with it at all. We spend our whole lives being molded by parents, by school, by friends and by whoever else gets ahold of our souls, and we get stuffed into a box that someone else built. We'll get ridiculed, redirected and labeled if we step away from the crowd.

I had hit a wall in my adulthood where becoming who I was meant to be - had to start with me undoing everything that everyone else had always wanted me to be.

This meant learning what I thought, what my opinions were, what my own thoughts were. This meant discovering what being a Christian looked like without the culture telling me what it looked like. This meant discovering what my own relationship with Jesus looked like without an audience.

I felt a peace rush over me that night. It was settling in my heart that for the first time in my life I was willing to be ridiculed, redirected and labeled. I had no control anyway.

I had finally reached the point where I threw my hands up and said, "Everyone else can have the playground. I am ready to jump from the picnic table."

SIX

October 8, 2016, I wrote this on my personal blog. I like to call it #UndoingTheDoing:

"Following Jesus is such a wild and crazy adventure. Whoever thinks being a Chris- tian is boring, clearly doesn't know what they're talking about.

The past couple of months have been interesting for me. The Lord has revealed some new layers of broken areas of my heart that need healing. He's so gentle and kind with our hearts, though.

I have so often found myself so frus- trated after experiencing a mountain top season, only to find myself back in the valley. Gosh. This used to make me so upset.

If only I could grip onto the mountain top a little longer … if only I could dig my heels in and hold on a little longer… but nonetheless – back to the valley I go.

I'm learning that my time spent on the

mountain top actually makes me long for the valley. I used to think that happiness was up there on top of the mountain, but it's not. The mountain top is a place of victory and rest AND much needed but we're not meant to stay there forever on this side of eternity.

In 2011, the hardest year of my life, I was plagued with anxiety that literally almost killed me. It was the darkest and hardest season of my life. When I was released from that season, I remember longing for that intimacy with Jesus again. I never wanted to return to those dark days – but once it was over, in an odd way I missed it.

Once I got past the initial shock of 'what the hell is happening to me?' and was forced to endure, I experienced a closeness with Jesus that I never experienced before. Anxiety is no joke. That season leveled me. It dropped me to the bottom of the bottom and I had to fully rely on Jesus day by day, hour by hour, minute by minute.

Once I emerged from that season I started a ministry to help other women overcome anxiety and depression. After 3 years of battling it out for other women's freedom, God asked me to release the ministry. I was heartbroken but I surrendered.

With the ministry (good works) out of the way and with a crushed heart, I realized there's a difference between healing and coping. Although God was healing me, I had learned to cope. Anxiety no longer controlled my life - but it was still very present, just manageable.

God started to pull back more layers in my heart and showed me deep wounds. My need for affirmation and validation was crippling. He walked with me through a year of intense surrender and learning about contentment. In one year, I experienced incredible grief and yet it was the most meaningful year I've lived thus far. It was like I discovered a whole new me - or more like the 'me' that has never been allowed to show herself.

I called that season #TheUndoing. It was where God stripped me down. He showed me so much disgusting stuff in my own heart and mind. He lavished me with love and grace and walked me through a season of releasing my dreams. During this season, I realized that we are taught our whole lives how to act, how to think, how to be - and then one day your eyes open and see clearly. What if I don't want to act, think, and be that way?! So, God had to undo a lot of wrong wiring.

Now this season - A word from God

while pumping gas, "You're done with this. You're moving on." This, meaning the constant lies of "you don't belong", "you don't fit." The Lord gave me a word that those were falling off of me. I was ecstatic for weeks.

I'm not gonna lie. For a second there – I thought I had arrived.

It was awesome to feel that way and yet at the same time terrifying because I know we NEVER arrive on this side of heaven.

And sure enough, I slid down that mountain top so dang fast and landed so hard in the valley that it knocked the air out of me and might have broken a few bones. I'm still not sure if I have internal bleeding or not.

So here I am. In the valley. Again. Except I don't try to resist the valley anymore. I trust that God knows what He's doing. He has proved Himself faithful so many times before and this time won't be any different.

I'm calling this season #UndoingTheDoing. As in, undoing the need to 'do' all the time. Create, post, write, share, encourage, dream, do, do, do. Yeah. I'm stopping that. I'm undoing the need to do. Not for forever. Just for a bit.

I don't hide the fact that I'm in

recovery. I'm a recovering people pleaser.

I've realized over the past few months that I have not been healed from people pleasing – I've just learned to cope.

When you take on mental/emotional abuse as a child/young adult, a person gets REALLY jacked up, y'all. Either you know that from your own experience ... or because you've met me and think I'm crazy. Sorry, not sorry. Emotional abuse in my past planted seeds in me that buried roots so darn deep. Emotional abuse, mental abuse, and trauma are not always big, scary things that happened (according to how the world looks at trauma), trauma and abuse can come from the way your mind perceives the world around you.

Just because a particular situation doesn't scare someone else doesn't mean it doesn't scare the hell out of you.

Look straight ahead. What you see is an accurate view of what's in front of you. Now, keep looking straight but tilt your head to where your chin is pointing toward your shoulder. You're now seeing the world through my lens. It's all off. It's skewed. It's tilted.

No matter how hard I try, I can't see the accurate view. Not yet. But I will.

It's great for creativity. It's great for writing. It's great for capturing the world from a different angle – but at the end of the day, it leaves you wondering 'what the heck is wrong with me?'

Being codependent in my past taught me to be an extreme people pleaser. I was told how to feel, how to act, how to think, how to be. I was told I wasn't good enough. I was called selfish. It was spoken over me that I believe the world owes me something. I was told I was a liar.

I had quickly learned to be what everyone else wanted me to be. When I was with my parents I tried my hardest to be their ideal 'April'. When I was with my friends – I was 'me'. I lied about everything with my parents to please them and tell them what they wanted to hear. If I performed well, I felt loved. If I slipped into 'me' mode, I felt like the love was taken away.

I became a master of people pleasing and living a double life. The problem with living a fake life and a real life is that eventually you forget which is which.

From 4th grade until I was 23 years old, I pleased everyone around me so I could feel love. If I ever started to think about myself or care for myself, I would be so afraid that someone would discover I was selfish, so I cared for others instead and never gave attention to my own needs, thoughts, desires, or voice.

From age 20 – 23ish, I was a professing follower of Jesus and was learning about boundaries. I was putting boundaries into practice and getting good at it.

At age 26 my whole world came crashing down because of anxiety. General Anxiety Disorder took my feet out from under me and left me in a deep depression.

Here I am today, free from GAD, clear with boundaries, but I feel like God is shining a spotlight on this people pleasing root. It's deep y'all.

I look back at my whole life and I see anxiety. I never even knew what the heck anxiety was until I was 26 and it tried to murder me. But looking back, anxiety is fear – and I have been fearful my whole life. Specifically, fearful of people not loving me.

Because of this fear, I have learned to be a really nice person. I have learned to do good things. I try my hardest not to step on toes. When I want to make good life decisions for myself that will better me, I feel like I'm wrong.

When people are mad, I feel like it's my fault. When someone has clearly wronged me, I think of some way how it might be my fault so I can let them off the hook.

If conflict is happening in front of me (that has nothing to do with me), I get extremely uncomfortable. I am so stinkin' naive sometimes. Because I was always called selfish and I know how bad that hurts, I refuse to call others selfish when they are straight up being selfish. People can butter me up with their words and drop me flat on my face with their actions – but because the words felt good, I totally miss the actions.

I've learned to doubt my thoughts and opinions and I get stuck when I'm trying to hold my ground – it's as if I forget what my position was on the matter or that I don't even care.

I don't fit because I won't let myself fit. I don't belong because I don't know how. I never feel good enough because I'm not perfect. I'm not looking with a straight view – I'm looking with a tilted view and I need God to do a chiropractic miracle up in here!

~

Why am I telling you all this? Well, for those of you who actually read this stuff, I wanted to explain before I just disappear.

I'm stepping away from social media until January 2017. My pages will still be active but I won't be there. I won't write on my blog during this time, I'll write privately.

I won't be attending many social events. It's not personal. I'm going to be very prayerful and specific about the events I do attend. So, if you message me and say, 'let's get coffee' and I decline, it's just a season and I hope you'll stick it out with me. Plus – I already know this is gonna be a MESSY season and I'm trying to protect you. You're welcome. ;o)

I have to find myself, y'all. I need to find that April that got suppressed many years ago. God knows where she's at and we're on a journey to rescue her. I need to know what she likes. What she doesn't like. I need to tell her that she's loved and wanted and able. She needs to know it's not her fault. She has a voice and it needs to be discovered. She's breaking free, you guys!

In 2011 my feet were knocked out from under me, I was tossed into the fire and I had to sit in the uncomfortable pain that comes with lack of control. To finish off 2016, I'm voluntarily walking into the furnace. It's going to suck – but I know that God is going to do something incredible. He never leads us where He isn't willing to go Himself.

I'm running hard after Jesus over these

next few months. I need to know what following Jesus looks like without the culture telling me what it looks like. I need to know what following Jesus looks like without an audience. No likes, comments, amens, etc. No affirmation.

If my fear is that people won't love me, I need to be led into a lonely place where I can see that people not loving me, is okay. People not seeing me, is okay. People not cheering me on, is okay. People not agreeing, is okay.

Jesus is enough. I don't want to go on idolizing what others think or really even caring what they think. I cannot serve two masters. Jesus is enough.

My doing is a manifestation of anxiety. It's an outlet for me to feel good and feel like I'm contributing good to this world. I need to learn what life looks like when I'm not doing. I need to be still and silent.

God always reveals things to our hearts at just the right time. The things I've shared here are so obvious now. But I've never seen them before now. Only by removing the doing, I see clearly.

~

This blog captures a pivotal breaking point in tearing down walls around my identity that kept anxiety alive in my life. The fear of not being able to hide behind projects, titles and good works was terrifying – but absolutely necessary if I was going to press forward to living a life of freedom.

SEVEN

I have always loved to gather women together for community. I guess because I've always felt like an outsider, I figured if I started my own group and knit people together, I'd know how to properly do it, because I long for community myself. Over the years I've led numerous small groups and gatherings for women.

One summer I hosted a couple of events on my friend's property in Franklin, Tennessee. The land was gorgeous. We could watch the sunset as we started worship during the event. As the evening rolled in, the sky would grow dark. We could see shooting stars. The environment was perfect for creating a space for women to put their focus on God. I was so grateful for this short season with these events.

Before the last gathering that I ever hosted on this property I had spent the past few hours fuming with anger. In four hours, I had to go teach women about the prodigal son and how God waits on us to return to him and then throws us a big party. I had spent weeks preparing for this event. I was ready to show the difference between the 'good' son and the prodigal son and how God makes room for both, when I found out that a friend of my friend, Shelly, was apparently mad at me.

Now, I have to tell you, I don't have friends who are mad at me. I have healthy relationships, with friends who talk to me if and when there is an issue or misunderstanding. I have friends who trust in my goodness and believe the best in me even if I rub them the wrong way. I have healthy friendships where agitation doesn't linger and grow. I have friendship with mature women. I have not had friends who are mad at me in years; not since I walked away from the dramatic friendships I once had many years ago.

I didn't really know Shelly's friend very well. Her name was Kayla. She didn't know me and I didn't know her; we just knew of each other. We had been around each other and shared mutual friends, but we didn't know each other personally. For some reason Kayla had never liked me. She never wanted to like me and always searched for a reason to hate me.

I was a master people pleaser, so there was never a reason for anyone to hate me. Even though Kayla didn't have a reason, she sat on the verge of hating me, waiting for her opportunity. That summer she found that opportunity. She had overheard a conversation between me and our mutual friend, Shelly, about her. The part that Kayla heard was completely out of context, but I can see how the conversation would have hurt her feelings, since she didn't know the full story.

On the day of the women's event, Shelly was confronted by Kayla, and Shelly called to tell me about their conversation. Ultimately, they had worked it out, but frankly Kayla was pissed at me and hated me.

I could feel the anxiety in my chest and the sickness in my stomach. I cannot have anyone hate me. That goes against all my master people pleasing skills. I must win Kayla back and change her mind about me. I don't want her to see me as this awful human being, because clearly, I'm not. She just needs to understand and hear my side, then she will understand and like me.

I reached out to Kayla via Facebook Messenger, starting with something along the lines of how sorry I was that she had overheard the conversation between me and Shelly. I could clearly see how she would be hurt, but let me explain and hopefully we can work this out.

Her response was anything but along the lines of working it out. She told me about myself. She cussed at me and called me fake and all the other things that a people pleaser can't dare to hear about themselves.

I stayed calm and tried to type up another sweet and gentle response to win her back over and explain my heart. One of my greatest fears is that someone would misunderstand my heart and not let me explain. Of course, it was one of my greatest fears; it's kryptonite for a people pleaser!

As I hit enter on my three paragraphs of please understand and see where I'm coming from and please don't hate me response, I received an immediate message that said, Kayla has blocked you. It was the hardest punch to the gut. She didn't let me explain.

She didn't want to work it out. She didn't want to hear my side. Kayla just wanted to be angry. She had always wanted to hate me and now she had found her reason.

I was so hurt. I cried like a child that just watched her dog get hit by a car.

I don't have people that are this immature in my life. I don't find myself explaining my heart very often because I don't have silly, petty people in my life that are angry and bitter and want to be victims in their lives, looking to hate me or anyone else. This is foreign in my world. I remember it from my high school days but not in my adulthood. The only reason why a conversation about this mutual friend was taking place was because my friend Shelly was struggling in the relationship with Kayla, and me as Shelly's friend was helping her process through the stickiness of their relationship based on all that Shelly had ever told me. I didn't know Kayla personally, I only knew what Shelly had told me.

I was blocked. Not only was there no reconciliation, I was cussed at, called names and blocked so I could not explain myself. There was absolutely nothing I could do. If Kayla wanted to hate me, she could hate me. It didn't matter how nice I was. It didn't matter how much I loved Jesus and how much I talked about him. It didn't matter how perfect I tried to be - if Kayla wanted to hate me, it was her choice. I couldn't change her mind.

That night I went to the gathering. I led the event. I taught about the prodigal son and prayed with the women who were requesting prayer, but I couldn't shake the pain that someone hated me and I had no control in this situation.

I made it through the event and drove home that night in tears. Sad tears, angry tears and lots of them. Kayla hating me pressed me right over the edge; and that's exactly where I needed to be.

It was on that ledge that another tiny death was waiting for me. This time it was to behead people pleasing, that image that I had of myself in my head, of trying to constantly stay in that mold, in that box. It was time to let go. Kayla's need to hate me shattered the self-image I had worked so hard to create. Being wounded by Kayla revealed another layer of deception in my heart.

I was good. At least, I wanted to believe I was good. If Kayla doesn't think I'm good, is this an absolute?

Kayla's negative opinion of me wrecked me. The opinion of someone I didn't even know held power over me. The opinion of someone who didn't care to know me or listen to me was dictating my mood and emotions. How could I give so much power to a person who held such an insignificant role in my life?

I wrestled with this situation for quite some time before I realized it was time to move on. I had to pick up the shattered pieces of her opinions and toss them out. Only I could allow her to have power over me. My problem wasn't with Kayla, my problem was with my need for Kayla's approval. She had created her perception of me and it wasn't enough. It wasn't good. Her action was to hate me.

My action was to keep pressing forward. But pressing forward meant more undoing.

Eight

The Lord had already been working on my heart and rearranging furniture in my soul. But all my performance and striving and good-Christian-girl motives crumbled this particular day with Kayla. I realized that no matter how good you are (or think you are), no matter how much you pursue peace among others – you still mess up and people can still choose to hate you.

I found myself so angry about this situation. I'm talkin' fuming! I was mad, y'all. But it was just what I needed to push me into a new place in my life.

For 2 days, I pretty much said nothing to anyone. I just didn't have words. I sat in silence and tears would flow. You ever feel that pain in your heart and there are no words … just tears? That's where I was. I felt bruised on the inside.

On day 3 I snapped. I was with my husband, sitting at The Juice Bar, sipping a green juice in silence when I finally opened my mouth and a flood of cuss words started flowing out. I was really pissed off. I was pissed off at everyone and everything. I was pissed off at church. Pissed off at ministry. Pissed off at friends. Pissed off about everything that revolved around serving Jesus and being in "community" with others.

All my efforts had left me really pissed off.

Tony, sitting in silence and listening to me rant - starts cracking up. I mean, I'm fuming and the guy starts laughing at me.

I wanted to be pissed off at him in that moment but instead I started laughing too. I was exhausted. Tony, with true compassion, looked at me and told me that he understood. He knew exactly what I was going through and it was actually refreshing to see me be human.

The next 5 days I isolated myself from the world (besides work) because I couldn't trust myself to not destroy anyone and everyone I came in contact with.

If I heard one more "I'm praying for you" or "God will get you through this" or had another scripture texted to me – I was going to lose it. I know people meant well. Hey, that's what we do as Christians. Honestly, you were damned if you did and damned if you didn't in this situation with me. Offer hope and support and I would bite your head off. Stay silent and I would be irritated that you didn't care. I didn't need to be fixed. I wasn't broken in this season. I mean, I was broken ... but not like that. I actually felt like I was busting out of the matrix! I knew if I told anyone I would be called a 'backslider' or judged because I was going against the Williamson County cultural Christian 'way'. I get it. I would have done the same thing to anyone else going through what I went through.

I didn't trust myself during those days.

I was a loose cannon.

Everything I had built up came crashing down. I didn't want to lead anymore. I didn't want to be a ministry leader, writer, or freedom advocate anymore. I didn't want to save people and strive for opportunities to share the gospel ... I just wanted to be April. Broken, messy, lover of Jesus, don't have all the answers, passionate, in process – April. I didn't want a platform. No audience. No "can you pray for me" messages.

Because for once I saw myself just the same as everyone around me... the same as those I had tried to reach and lift up. I realized I am that person too. I don't have answers. I'm no better or higher leveled than anyone else!

Years ago, I created myself as a leader. I created myself as a woman after God's heart. I painted the picture exactly how I wanted and I was tired.

I remember sitting on my patio one night alone in silence. Staring at the stars, tears filling my eyes from the unexplainable pain I felt in my core. I thought, *'This is not freedom.'* So, I said to The Lord, "Jesus! This is not freedom. This is not what you died for. I believe in freedom but this is not it. Take me back to that simple place with you before the striving and the doing and the going and all these works. All this pressure and 'look at me' and feeling guilty for not acting/doing/being good/ nice enough ... or praying enough or reading my Bible enough or quoting scriptures perfectly ... I missed something along the way and I'm desperate for the freedom that you speak about."

Nine

Y ou guys – I was a heathen hot mess for those few days. My thoughts and words were awful. I was so mad. I was not put together. I was not nice. Yet, God sat right there with me. He let me be a horrible person (I consider it horrible for me ... and for all "I knew better.") I was ugly and He came close. My ugliness didn't scare Him away.

His goodness has nothing to do with my goodness. He's good because He's God and that's His very nature. He's good when I'm not good. He's good when I royally screw things up. He's good when things don't go my way or when I'm not on my best behavior. He's good when I yell at my kids or act bratty with my husband. He's good just because.

His goodness, grace and love isn't tied to our wretchedness. No, it just covers it. I cannot understand that type of goodness but I know it exists. I know He offers it over and over again.

Thirteen years ago, I went to church and fell in love with Jesus – or so I thought. In actuality, I went to church and fell in love with church.

I saw women leaders in the church and realized if I could be as good as them – I was on the right track. If I could hang out in their groups, I was on the right track. If I could speak their language and pray pretty prayers like them – oh yeah, I was on the right track.

This leaves you empty.

Thirteen years ago, I did go to church and fall in love with church ... but a few months ago I sat on my patio with Jesus, completely broken and really pissed off and realized somewhere along the way I fell in love with Jesus and HE was all I wanted ... and I was willing and wanting to give up everything just to have him.

No more lights and smoke machines. No more 'look at me' moments posted to social media. No more "community" that was really just meeting for coffee every once in a while, texting and/or Facebooking with each other (In Jesus' name of course). No more showing up to Sunday services packaged nicely.

Just desperate for Jesus.

And I heard Him say to me, "All I ever wanted was you. Right where you are. Not where 'they' are - but where you are. I can do more with who you are than I can with who you think you're supposed to be."

"What! Jesus? You mean ... you want *This*? You want the April who totally loves you and wants to live her life for you but still cusses sometimes and can be extremely selfish?

You want this girl who doesn't always have the best disciplines? This scattered-brain, loner? You want this person whose natural gift is *not* hospitality ... more of a taker than a giver ... You want that! Me? Who struggles to trust people? The me who can actually be extremely critical?"

Romans 12:3 flooded my mind: *"For by the grace given me I say to every one of you: Do not think of yourself more highly than you ought, but rather think of yourself with sober judgment, in accordance with the faith God has distributed to each of you."*

I still don't understand how God can love me right where I am. I thought I was doing a pretty darn good job letting God love me where I thought I should be. I realized that striving was never about God's approval. It was about people's approval. It was more about where the church culture says we should be as individuals rather than where God says we should be.

I may not understand his love but I know I feel it.

And because I have let him meet me where I'm at ... where I'm truly at ... love and grace meet me daily (moment by moment, second by second). I'm living under an awareness of his love and grace and how I don't deserve it and yet he keeps pouring it out.

Fear vanishes.

Anxiety flees.

When you experience that kind of love ... When you accept – Hey! Here I am. Here's where I am today. Am I still loveable? And He says you are... The hurt and The Healer collide.

You are changed forever.

You cannot receive this kind of love without wanting to let it pour out of you and onto others.

It's just too powerful. It's transformational love.

We don't have to strive to be good Christians. What the heck is a good Christian anyway? Who put the 'good' in front of Christian. If you love Jesus, just be a Christian. A devoted follower of Jesus Christ – in process. And if you don't love Jesus - be a nice human.

We're quick to say "Oh, I know we don't arrive until we get to heaven" and yet we expect everyone who claims to love Jesus to *not* be in process. To not be messy. To not speak out of line. And Heaven forbid – to not miss a Sunday church service.

(Not to be confused with accountability... there's definitely a place for that.)

That's what following Jesus is ... 'Look – I'm a freakin' hot mess express and I'm in desperate need of a Savior!" Right? I'm not who I was 10 years ago (Thank God!). I won't be the same 10 years from now (I'm sure I'll be saying 'Thank God' again then).

In the scriptures, Jesus met the Samaritan woman at the well. She was a hot mess express too. He went out of his way, broke cultural rules and met her where she was. Her encounter with Jesus changed her. Yeah, He called her out in love ... but he didn't box her in with a list of rules and regulations. He didn't rub her face in her shortcomings. He met her where she was. He loved her where she was. However, she didn't stay where she was because her encounter with His love changed her.

I believe the thought of bypassing rules and regulations of cultural Christianity leads people to believe you're condoning bad behavior ... as long as you love Jesus.

That's not what I'm saying at all. Jesus met the woman at the well but that same Jesus flipped tables in the temple. Jesus will never condone sin. Never.

I get that.

Behavior change comes from heart change. Change doesn't take place with good acting skills. It comes from a rewiring of the heart and mind.

Jesus touched the leper. Disease stricken people. Lepers had to ring bells and yell "Unclean!" as they walked through the town so that they wouldn't accidentally touch anyone else. Jesus walked right up and touched the leper. Jesus isn't afraid of your mess. Your mess doesn't rub off on Him. He rubs off on you.

This is Who I'm in love with. This is Who I want to chase after all the days of my life.

This.

This. Is. Freedom. His name is Jesus.

I share this discovery in my journey because I was unaware how much anxiety I was experiencing from constantly feeling like I was not doing this 'follow Jesus thing' correctly. I didn't feel good enough prior to giving my life to Him and I certainly didn't feel good enough once I publicly confessed my love for Him.

I wasn't mimicking the Jesus I saw in scriptures. I was mimicking the idea of what I thought being a Christian was based on those I saw around me. If anyone from the Christian faith ever tried to manipulate or control me, the worst thing they could have ever done was tell me to read my Bible.

I don't say all this to speak negatively of other Christians. Yeah, some have really let me down but I can only think of how often I meant well but let others down as well. I had friendships in the past that went up in flames. Upon our friendship breakup, they told mutual friends that they actually felt free once I wasn't in their life anymore. I don't deny this or blame them for this. I now know I was self-righteous. The humbling part is I was completely unaware until way after the fact.

Wherever humans are there will be messiness - because humans are messy. This includes you and this definitely includes me.

My friend Melissa asked me a simple question during the time I was having the major epiphany about who I was as a follower of Jesus.

"I can't keep up. I can't keep being what everyone wants me to be. I can't keep going and performing and leading and guiding. I just can't be all these things anymore. I just want to move away and get away from everyone so I can start all over." I said in my dramatic tantrum tone that she's used to hearing during my meltdowns.

She listened intently and calmly responded with a question that would set me free.

"Who asked you to be this way?"

Her question irritated me. I didn't realize the power it held in the moment. Instead, I felt irritated and offended. This simple question was one I couldn't answer with a list of names. I could only drop my head, endure the fire in my chest and respond with, "No one."

We sat in silence. I took a deep breath, lifted my head and met her eyes with mine. "No one, Melissa. No one has asked me to be this way. Only me."

Realizing I had locked myself in a prison of anxiety that only I could free myself from all along was humbling. The deep-rooted need to perform and be all that everyone else wanted me to be was actually just a byproduct of me trying to prove to myself that I was enough. No one else cares.

Yeah, we'll have naysayers and haters in our lives but trust me, no one else cares about how good you are or good you are not because they are too busy obsessing over how they're not enough. They're obsessing over what they think everyone else thinks of them. Convincing themselves that they don't care what others think while all along suffocating under the need to be better.

My friend T.J., the training manager at the behavioral health company I work for says it best.

"The only obstacle you're facing is the one you're creating. Stop it."

These are very similar words that I shared with a teammate the other day. She was frustrated. Her job is to help people struggling with addiction get into treatment. Her father struggles with a pain pill addiction and has never gotten help. She was trying to help a young lady overcome obstacles to get into a high-quality treatment program that was not state funded. The girl, who called my teammate for help, was now reluctant to go to treatment. The girl was scared. My teammate started freaking out about how she was failing to help people. I let her have space to be frustrated and defeated and then abruptly said to her, "Jess! You are your greatest obstacle. You can do this. You just have to get out of your own way."

As quickly and sharp as I spoke the words outward, they bounced off of her and shot right back into me. The majority of our freak out moments are just us getting in our own way. We are creating obstacles that didn't exist before we put them there on our path.

I don't truly believe the church communities I've been a part of ever tried to make me join a cult (well, maybe one… but it's irrelevant now). I don't think the people were trying to make me be like them because they were actually too busy trying to be like everyone else. Everyone seems to be following someone who doesn't even know where they're going. I was no different.

Religion is tricky. I thought I was spiritual but didn't realize how much religion I had strapped to my ankles, holding me down. I thought I signed up for freedom when I gave my heart to Jesus. He offered freedom but I picked up bondage to performance, wanting to belong and wanting to fit instead. I traded one set of chains for another because fear was owning me. Instead of living carelessly in the world, I was now living under expectations of who and how I was supposed to be as a Christian. My bondage was not a church issue, it was a me issue. The anxiety I experienced was yet again embedded in the people pleasing parts of my own heart and the fear of being found out.

TEN

In the scripture Jesus said, "Follow Me." He didn't say, "Follow those who follow me."

On my journey of following Jesus, I found myself submerged in Christian language, disciplines and ideas ... but felt very far from the heart of Jesus.

I felt The Lord was asking "Who are you following, April?". I got honest with myself and realized I wasn't following Jesus. I was following the idea of Jesus among a heavy Christian culture. Upon this revelation, He simply said, "Come. Follow me."

As I read the scriptures and followed Jesus throughout the Word, I realized that a lot of what my life reflected was not what His reflected. When was the last time I had ever sat with someone who was going through a real crappy time and didn't try to fix them with scriptures but actually listened and was present in the discomfort with them? When was the last time I listened to understand and not to respond with some Christian cookie-cutter response? Because that's exactly what Jesus did. He pulled up a chair with the messy and broken.

I was convicted and humbled. I had missed the mark for quite some time. Perfect Love that casts out fear is hard to obtain when you're not chasing Perfect Love, but instead chasing approval, comfort and popularity.

It makes me tear up now. He is freedom. Simply, Jesus. I have tasted and seen that the Lord is good, just because He is.

ELEVEN

Three months passed away from the public social media eye after my meltdown. Below is the first blog I wrote upon my return:

"12 years of following Jesus and I hit a crossroads.

I can't do this anymore. This Christian 'Leader' – *let me teach you something and lead you* – thing.

Leading ministry, hosting Bible Study, Online Bible Studies, Coffee Shop Bible Study, Church Small Groups, Worship Events, Prayer Events ... bleh. I. Just. Can't.

I just got burnt out with creating social media platforms and giving you a view into a life that's painted with pretty words and pictures. What you see out there is real for me but the beauty in writing is that you can always edit and clean it up before you present it ... unlike the me you see in real time. The unedited and not so cleaned up, April.

The one who doesn't always say or do or feel the right things.

Unedited. Unpolished. Raw. What you see is what you get.

Me.

How do you bring you to this social media highlight world? … Where everyone is claiming to be real and authentic … but are we really? Can you even be real when we're connecting deeper on the internet than we are face to face?

Here goes my social media tangent:

I pray that God continues to use the platform of social media to share the Good News for those He has equipped and called to use it. I'm sure there's different seasons for every person.

I'm just in a really weird place with it all.

Just a few ramblings from my time away from social media:

*I realized I could think. I'm an extrovert so I process by talking (or writing) and social media has always been a great outlet. But when the outlet was gone and the platforms were gone – I realized I had thoughts.

Beautiful thoughts. Deep thoughts.

There was just something about the stillness of sitting at a red light without checking my phone … or waiting in a drive-thru line and not checking my phone. Being present with my thoughts was extremely strange and wonderful to me.

*Anxiety vanished and I had more energy. I felt like a left the party and went home to rest. All this information wasn't smacking me in my face constantly. People WAY outside of my sphere of influence who were eating pasta, or getting their nails done, or someone's baby had strep throat, or this person was diagnosed with cancer, or that person's house burned down, another shooting, another injustice.

I'm a rescuer, people. Do you know what that negative information overload does to a rescuer-doer? Makes me have high anxiety in the backdrop of my life by showing me how I can't reach everyone and save everyone.

When the window is open too wide, we can see more reality than our hearts (or mental state) can handle. (I work in the addiction recovery and mental health field. I get enough of the open window on a day to day basis.)

The fear of what could happen to our children, spouse or loved ones can keep us so distracted that we don't even spend precious, present time with our loved ones.

Honestly, if it's outside of my sphere of influence, I can certainly pray and sometimes offer financial support - but it was draining my energy and taking away from those whom God has put right in front of me.

*My kids are no longer a burden. I can't tell you how many times I've told one or both of my kids to 'hold on' or 'give me a sec' or have even snapped and said, 'WHAT?!!' when heaven forbid they wanted my attention and I was too busy scrolling on social media.

I'm not proud of this. It's actually one of the most heartbreaking realizations that I had over the past three months.

My kids were in the way. They were in the way of my dreams and my to-do lists. They were in the way of me helping save souls for Jesus!

The scary thing is - I spent time with my kids and never knew I thought they were a burden. We always had family time and hang out time but I wasn't present. I was physically present but not mentally present. I would spend time with them during the day in anticipation for bedtime so I could write or do something for Jesus!

When I silenced everything around me for the past 3 months, my heart started to break because I felt like I saw Trinity and Sway for the first time.

Their whole lives have been plastered on social media. The past three months there weren't a lot of pictures because I was too busy being fully present with them. If there were pictures I sent them to grandparents, close friends and family through text messages.

I am so grateful for this eye-opening season while my babies are nine and three …. instead of having this realization when they are older.

*People move on when you leave the party. I'm not mad about it and there are no hard feelings. Me leaving social media wasn't a cry for attention by any means but the outcome was very interesting.

The people you think will reach out – don't reach out.

The people you least expect to reach out – reach out.

But … life goes on without you.

When everyone is at the party and you're at the party – it's easy.

When everyone is at the party and you leave the party, and go down the street – it's not so convenient anymore. Out of sight, out of mind. And I don't blame anyone … I'd move on too.

I'm sure some people back off out of

respect for the sabbatical – but either way, your phone grows silent and people move on.

I'm sure people would miss my posts and maybe be bummed for a little bit if I never returned to social media …. but life goes on with or without you. This was another beautiful discovery.

And not in some bitter way. I wasn't sitting around keeping count on who did and didn't reach out.

It was such a freeing realization though. I wasn't even sure how to return or if I would return. I came back … ish. I know I can never go fully back because my eyes have been opened and I lived real life for three months and plan to keep on living it.

Social media is not bad or evil. It's a tool. Just like any other tool – used properly and it's great, used incorrectly and it can become a weapon that brings harm. You just have to know yourself and what brings good and what brings harm. Each person is different.

I guess I'll end here for tonight since I seemed to have made this post mostly about my time away from social media. That should be enough to digest for one session, right?

I will say this. I've kept up with

Time-hop over the past three months (Time-hop is an app that shows you a list of all your social media postings on 'this day' 1 year ago, 2 years ago, and so on) and I know I'm not that person anymore. Some of those posts go back to 10 years ago. I get to see myself as an oversharing -hot mess 7-10 years ago, and then as a know-it-all Christian leader (Pharisee) 1-6 years ago.

I'm none of those things. I am just a follower of Jesus who is in process and will be in process for the rest of my life.

And that's okay.

These past 3 months were extremely humbling. I will never be the same. This season in the valley changed everything.

Everything.

I'll share more over time.

Oh - the picture on this blog (A picture was posted of me and my two children sleeping on the couch). I almost forgot. This picture popped up on Timehop a few days ago and I saved it on my phone.

You may see a precious mama napping with her babies - but I see an exhausted, busy woman. I see a little girl who was begging her mama to hang out. I see a baby who was clingy that day.

Then there was stillness.

I remember feeling depleted that day. My house was a mess. I didn't feel pretty.

There were 15,000 other things I wanted to do. Instead, I sat on the couch holding Sway. Trinity came and cuddled up beside me, just wanting to be close.

And in that stillness, we all fell asleep. My true ministry (my family), the one God put in my hands, the one I didn't have to strive for or fight for or make myself be known for... right there beside me in the stillness.

No performance. No doing.

Nothing BIG. Just being.

Just me in real time.

The unedited and not so cleaned up, April.

The one who doesn't always say or do or feel the right things.

~

It was freeing to finally walk out of that season in the valley and say, "Here I am! Love me or hate me. Take me or leave me – but this is all I got! "And truly be okay with it. The ideas of who I was supposed to be as a wife, mom, friend, worker, and Christian was suffocating me. Trying to keep people from hating me, just to find out they can still hate me was crushing. Constantly being busy with social media as a reminder of how badly I was missing the mark was causing unnecessary stress in my life. For once, I was pressing forward and claiming my freedom. I was learning to take my life back, or more so – I was learning to live my true life for the first time.

TWELVE

A couple of years ago, during the season when I worked with Dr. Brooks, as I would emotionally come undone he would help me process and press forward. He helped me recognize patterns in my life. I was finally realizing that the people keep changing, the environment keeps changing, but the problems remain the same. These brick-wall struggles I kept smashing into were wearing me out. I was the common denominator. These patterns were my problem. They were a reflection of something deeper that was going on inside of me.

It was easier to blame the outside world. To be honest, I thought it was the outside world. As much as it hurt to know I was the source of my own problem, I knew that by identifying the problem and me as the source, I could move towards healing.

One day, Tony and I were having coffee. We were processing being the common denominator of your own issues.

I said, "I feel like this same train keeps being sent my way and I just naturally get right on it and take a ride. I recognize the train now. I don't want to keep getting on it. I'm going to let it pass by."

Tony responded, "I believe there are three things the train offers and if we inherit any or all of those three, we get on the train and go on a ride of destruction. But if we can pass those things up by asking ourselves three questions, the train moves on and we are unshakable." I was curious. I'm a wordy person - an extroverted intuitive feeler. Tony is not. Tony is an introverted sensing thinker, according to the Myers Briggs personality test. Tony has a way of taking all the words that get jumbled up in my heart and mind, condensing them into what my friend Brandi calls "the Twitter version" (140 characters or less), and releasing them right into my heart as if they were an incredibly sharp spear. Tony broke it down like this:

1. Are you staying in your lane?
2. Are you comparing?
3. Are you being entitled?

Told you. Straight up Twitter version. When Tony speaks it packs a punch. He's an introvert. He doesn't waste words on nonsense and you can believe when he speaks he has put much thought into the words.

I admire introverts; especially Tony.

Tony was so right. I thought about earlier that week, when I was driving on the interstate on my way home from work. There was a place on the journey home where the lanes went from four lanes to two. This always caused a bottleneck and unnecessary stopping. One day I thought if I put on my break as the lanes start running out, maybe people will start merging over before the lane is completely gone and the traffic will keep moving instead of coming to a standstill.

I tested my theory. I could see in the distance the lanes were ending so I started pressing my break to allow cars to come over in front of me. Except the cars did not take the opportunity to merge over with a gaping space between me and the other car in front of me. Instead, the cars raced down the lane that was ending, causing a bottleneck, which led to a traffic jam.

I was so frustrated.

I've created an opening for them and they're not taking it! They'd rather fight and squeeze in from the lane that is ending.

It was in this moment that I realized I had created a solution to something I see as a problem and expected everyone else to be on board. I couldn't control the other cars. I could create a solution and extend it to those who want it, but I couldn't force anyone to adopt my idea. I was so focused on what the other cars were doing in the other lane, that I lost sight of my own. When we don't stay in our own lane, we start trying to dictate what everyone else is doing. I would have less stress and lower blood pressure if I'd just turn my radio up, relax and stay in my own lane. Let the other cars do what they do. Let them race and honk and make hand gestures at each other over there. Me, I'll be over here owning my own lane. I want to arrive refreshed, minding my own business and not angry because of what everyone else was doing on the journey.

In a world where social media dominates our social status, comparison is inevitable and if we don't keep a tight grip on letting our minds drift down the comparison path, we're in great danger. Comparison tries to steal our identities. Comparison tries to rub our faces in deep shame. Oh, and it will if we let it.

Comparison tells us we're not enough. There's not enough. We could do better. We could have more. We look at social media highlights and compare them to our low lights. We strive to do more, be more, give me, go more, buy more, more

more more. This path will leave you empty and exhausted. Entitlement tells us we deserve something and have the right to something. It tells us to set the bar really high and then raise it higher. We're left unsatisfied and pissed off because we all know life doesn't work this way. You don't always get what you think you should have, and even if you get it, it's not enough and you want something else that you think you deserve.

Any time I'm feeling unhappy and unsatisfied, I wonder if I've gotten on the train of destruction. I'll take myself down this quick checklist:

1.　Am I staying in my lane?
2.　Am I comparing?
3.　Am I being entitled?

When I'm feeling frustrated and deep dissatisfaction, I can usually answer yes to one or more of these questions. The cool thing is once you identify you're on the train, you can choose to keep riding or you can choose to get off.

The first time you let the train pass or decide to get off, you may experience anxiety stemming from fear. Well, of course! You're moving into new territory. You're breaking a pattern. The fear you feel is fueling the launch.

Stand firm and endure the discomfort of letting the train pass.

~

Changing your location doesn't change your situation if the problem lies within yourself. I remember feeling like drama and chaos always followed me wherever I went. I have come to the conclusion that if the location and the people keep changing and you keep having the same problems, there is one common denominator. It's you. The common denominator to my problems was me.

Have you been on the train of destruction for far too long? Who knew the way to get off the train is to just get off? It's that simple. You may have to get off multiple times before you stay off - but the first step is recognizing you're the problem, you're on the train, and you can get off.

THIRTEEN

Ihave nothing but gratitude for the messy and broken parts of my story.

There is no part of your story that cannot be used for good. We just have to stop resisting the pain. We have to stop resisting the discomfort of life and learn to embrace it ... all of it. I believe with all my heart that Jesus came to give us abundant life – on this side of eternity.

This is why I had a meltdown in the fall of 2016. I was sitting on my balcony, staring out into the night sky, pissed off at the world and thought, "This *is not freedom. This is not abundant life. This is not what You died for, Jesus."* Then I spent the next 3 months discovering true freedom through Christ that changed my entire being. .

Jesus didn't come to give you a boring, worrisome, tiring, bitter life. He came to give you a life of freedom and abundance in the midst of this messed up hell-hole world we live in! He came to show you secrets that pour out of his nature. He came to lavish you in love that can't be contained ... so you pour it out on others because it's so rich and merciful and too good not to give away!

He came to give you joy in the middle of deep sorrow. He came to give you hope in the midst of what seems like hopeless situations. He came to give you great courage when your knees are shaking and fear feels big.

And He's still here.

We're missing Him moment by moment. Day by day. Completely missing Him. Being so wrapped up in the troubles of the world. Silly and petty stuff that means nothing.

We get caught in hating our job but then get a new job and wind up hating that job too. Complaining. Being a gossip. Hating our boss' decisions and think we have better answers to all the company's problems.

We're angry at our spouse. They're never good enough or do enough. We're constantly picking out the negatives about them instead of speaking life into them and praising them for all they are and all they do.

We're upset about never having enough money when in fact we're just not budgeting and managing money properly.

We complain about our health, but do nothing to enhance our health.

Distracted, busy, down and out. Completely missing the beauty in what we think is just another mundane, boring day when in all actuality, it's another chance at life.

2016 I left the ministry role of 'teacher'. I don't write this to teach or preach. I write this to tell you what I know to be true. I write this because I was once damaged goods until Jesus picked me up and said, "No. You're just good."

You are not damaged goods. You are just good. You were made by the Creator and He says you're good. All that He has made is good.

The broken and messy segments of our lives are not who we are. Those are just fragmented pieces that allow God's glory to shine through us. Trust me, you don't want to NOT have those pieces. Those very shreds of your life create the breeding ground for miracles.

If you are consumed in shame and guilt at this moment you need to know that you are deeply loved. Yes. Even if you did that thing (whatever that thing is). There may be real consequences and there may be real pain associated with whatever that thing is ... but that never takes away from the fact that you are deeply loved.

If you are overwhelmed with your past. You can be free from it. God is wondering why you're still holding on to it and allowing it to steal your abundant life from you. Hand that over to Him. However, you need to do that ... just hand it over and don't carry that with you anymore.

If you are drowning in anxiety, worry, fear – you may have a control problem. You want to be in control and know the outcome of everything. I know, because I'm recovering from control, myself.

Your battle is not against anxiety. Your battle is in your resistance to go to God when anxiety rears its ugly head.

If you are flat out in a place of complete defeat and pain. Real, deep, pain. Only you understand it. It's that type of pain that knocks the breath out of you. Where you have no words and even when you try to talk about it – it doesn't make sense out loud.

If you're in that place - my heart is with you. It's the place where there are no real answers. Heck, you're not even sure you're looking for an answer and you actually get annoyed when people offer an answer. Answers are stupid at this point. Do you know that place of pain? I don't really have words of comfort for you because I know there are no words of comfort, there is only The Comforter. He sees you and His heart breaks when your heart breaks. He is there with you. He heals the brokenhearted and binds up their wounds. He truly does. I'm sorry you're going through this.

Ugh. Those seasons suck. Beauty is birthed from them but while you're in the middle of them they just straight up *suck*.

So, all of this rambling to say – God is good. Even when we're not good.

He's good.

There is beauty in the pain of life. Your story is still being written and it's not over yet.

Look for Jesus among you. Don't just make Him be at church only. Blah. That's boring. The Kingdom of God is among us. Wake up to that! He's playing the best ever scavenger hunt game with you but you haven't showed up! He's waiting.

Seek God consistently on how to love and mentor your children but don't be so hard on yourself when you totally screw them up!

Know when to draw hard lines and set boundaries to take care of yourself and be present in the moment.

If you're not living an abundant life – you're choosing to live a life that was never intended for you. I know it can be confusing if I throw all this out at you and tell you, 'oh, but I don't have the answer for you.' I don't have the answer but I will always offer hope.

My story is packed full of hope. Your story offers hope. When we share our stories we connect with another human and say, "me too." We rise up when we know that someone else has overcome what we're going through. We love the beauty from ashes stories but boy, we sure hate living in the ashes.

I hear about ashes every day working in addiction treatment. Every now and then I get to put my management job aside and pick up the role of a Treatment Specialist. These are the first real heroes on the front lines of addiction treatment. They are the ones who answer the phone and talk to people struggling with addiction and/or their heartbroken family/loved ones. Treatment Specialists are like the paramedics. They arrive on the accident scene first and try to get the situation stabilized long enough to rush the patient to the hospital.

It's a raw, messy job.

There are countless times when a team member has approached me after a hard phone call, with tears in their eyes - needing a moment to take a walk and leave the building.

I've had a team member meet me in the middle of the admissions floor, fall into my arms and weep because someone she was working with kept dragging their feet, delaying treatment and died because of an overdose.

I've had team members spot me with tears in my own eyes, my heart breaking from a conversation with a family who is begging me to help their child. My team will love on me. They will not let you ache alone. These are the folks I get to stand and battle with every day.

One day at work, deep in the trenches, I got to help a family move mountains to get a young man in treatment. It was well worth the fight and well worth the long hours. This war we wage against addiction, although painful at times, is well worth the fight. Sometimes it feels like we are fighting an uphill battle but that doesn't mean we stop fighting. We lose to the disease of addiction. We lose a lot. But we win also. We win a lot. Because we believe in the beauty from ashes stories and find continuous hope in how often we win.

I've been taught well by a team of incredible Treatment Specialists. Yeah, I help manage ... but I'm constantly learning from them more than they'll ever learn from me. I can't help but overflow with gratitude for the soldiers I get to battle addiction beside in this season of my life. These warriors who dust off the residue on those who are broken.

Many of the folks I work with have emerged from ashes themselves. They get the need for hope. They get it. I hear them share the shattered pieces of their stories. Brokenness meets brokenness without judgement. It's in that place where a seed of hope gets planted in the person on the other end of the telephone.

I often find my own story right there in the midst of theirs. I realize we are not as separate as I've always thought we were. I can see that it's not about avoiding your messiness, afraid that you might rub off on me. I want you to rub off on me and I want to leave tear stains on you. Because only in that place do we know we've experienced true human connection, hope and love.

My own fears being unraveled right there in the midst of their fears. Anxiety flows through me but I envelope anxiety with courage. The bravery and courage to keep pressing forward is not the easy route. It's surely the road less traveled because we don't want to move through the discomfort. We want to check out, numb, abort, or cover but we do not, by any means, we do not want to move through those feelings.

One of my favorite authors, Jon Acuff dropped a line that I'd love to steal but I have to give credit where credit is due - "Bravery is a choice, not a feeling. You can't wait until you feel brave enough to do something." Joyce Meyer says, "Do it afraid."

I say, keep pressing forward.

My whole life, up until this point has been about mimicking, creating, doing, becoming, performing and presenting anything but my true self. I was incredibly fearful that my true self would not be enough. I'm learning that there is nothing wrong with our true selves, in fact people are craving to share their true selves - heck, people are craving to meet and discover their true selves because we've been running and hiding from it our whole lives. For me, this fear of being found out was the ultimate root of deception that was causing anxiety to plague me for so many years.

Our weaknesses unite us. Our stories of hope in the midst of our suffering unite us. I'll close this chapter with these powerful words from scripture. Paul, a follower of Jesus, shares that he has a 'thorn in his flesh'. No one really knows what this thorn is - but we do know it torments him and that Paul begged God to take it away three times.

"Three times I pleaded with the Lord to take it away from me. But he said to me, "My grace is sufficient for you, for my power is made perfect in weakness." Therefore, I will boast all the more gladly about my weaknesses, so that Christ's power may rest on me. That is why, for Christ's sake, I delight in weaknesses, in insults, in hardships, in persecutions, in difficulties. For when I am weak, then I am strong." 2 Corinthians 12:8-10 NIV

~

Check out The Message version:

"At first, I didn't think of it as a gift, and begged God to remove it. Three times I did that, and then he told me, My grace is enough; it's all you need. My strength comes into its own in your weakness."

Once I heard that, I was glad to let it happen. I quit focusing on the handicap and began appreciating the gift. It was a case of Christ's strength moving in on my weakness. Now I take limitations in stride, and with good cheer, these limitations that cut me down to size—abuse, accidents, opposition, bad breaks. I just let Christ take over! And so, the weaker I get, the stronger I become."

Debilitating anxiety lost its grip in my life but fear shows up from time to time. Maybe some consider it a 'thorn' but I just think it's a very real part of our human existence. If we coward back behind fear, we lose. If we keep pressing forward even when fear feels crippling, we win. Perfect Love casts out all fear. Perfect Love doesn't keep fear from showing up, but it does cast it out if we choose to embrace who we are, live reckless with grace, love wholeheartedly ...

... and, no matter what, we keep pressing forward.

FOURTEEN

Writing this book was quite a process. I tried to write this book back in 2005 but I picked up my journal and began to write; "My name is April. I was born on March 14, 1985 in Ardmore Oklahoma…" After pondering on my next sentence for what seemed like 15 minutes, I shut my journal. I just didn't have much to write about at 20 years old.

In 2011 during my season with anxiety, I felt like I was going to write a book about the whole experience one day, but I didn't know when. I started blogging in 2011, but blogged from a stance of 'I am already healed.'

In 2012, I started writing this book, except it wasn't this book. It was called Pressing Forward. I wrote it over a five-year span. I wrote it, rewrote it, lost my flash drive (twice), found my flash drive (twice), edited the book, wrote it again, when in October of 2016 I finally turned it into a publisher. At that point, I felt that I just needed to actually finish the book and turn it in. Fear was present because I realized I was afraid of the rejection. If I never turned the book in, I didn't have to worry about it being rejected.

That October night my family was sleeping. I was at the kitchen table finishing my proposal. I finished the book, the proposal and I sent my work to the publisher. I knew that if a publisher doesn't respond within a couple of weeks, it means they weren't interested in your work. That night when I turned in my book I knew that I had pressed through to a whole new level in life. I not only finished a large project but I had put my work out there to be rejected. This alone was enough. I didn't need my book to be published. I just needed to know I could finish and take the risk of being critiqued or even worse - rejected. I felt accomplished. The only reason I had this kind of courage was because of all the sifting and breaking down that God had done in my life over the past few years — starting with a panic attack that was triggered by a chest-cold.

The months went on and I never heard from the publisher. I knew my work had been rejected and I moved on.

In summer of 2017 an old friend, Sarah M. (a different Sarah than the one from the beginning of this book) reached out and asked could we meet to talk. It was so great to see her and catch up. We move through the 'how have you been' small talk when I finally asked her, "So what's up? Why did you want to meet?"

Her eyes filled with tears. She said, "I know you've had your own battle with anxiety and I was just hoping to meet and hear some of your story, tell some of mine, and draw out some hope."

Sarah and I shared our stories back and forth. She shared where she was and I shared where I had been. We talked for hours catching up and encouraging one another. I think she left feeling less alone and less crazy, and I left feeling encouraged by her - even in what she saw as one of her darker hours, messy, torn, broken - I was encouraged by her.

She didn't have to be put together to be effective. Actually, her brokenness is what encouraged me. The fact that she had reached out to talk. The fact that she pulled herself out of bed that morning. The fact that she was alive in front of me. The very fact that she let herself be vulnerable in front of me. I gave her permission to be right where she was without trying to fix her. She had reached out to me to help her, but she had no idea how much she actually helped me.

I remember months before when I was praying through my identity junk after Kayla decided to hate me and I had come apart.

Just like months before when I heard the Lord say to me in regard to my performance and perfectionism issues; "I can do more with who you are than I can with who you think you're supposed to be."

I needed to be okay with authenticity. I needed to be okay with not fitting the plastic, Christian action-figure of who I thought I needed to be, mimicking the powerful Christian women around me - or the idea of the powerful Christian women around me, because in all actuality, they're a hot mess too.

Sarah bringing herself, right where she was, to our meet-up wrecked me for the good. The courage that it takes to reach out for help and then crumble during conversation is admirable. The next day I felt I should give Sarah my manuscript for the Pressing Forward book. I wasn't doing anything with it and instead of it sitting and rotting away, I figured it could help encourage someone. I sent her the manuscript and asked her to please not steal it or publish it for herself.

As I read back through the first chapter, familiarizing myself with the book I had written for five years, but not read or touched in eight months, I thought about resending it to the publisher. I wanted them to tell me why they rejected it. Without thinking too much about it, I sent my work back over to the publisher, asking them to reconsider publishing the book.

That same day the publisher responded stating he had never seen the book. He did not remember ever getting the book the previous fall. I sent my book and proposal back to him, and he accepted it for publishing.

I am so extremely grateful the book was accepted. It's an incredible honor to be able to publish a book, but as I spoke with the publisher, I shared that after working in behavioral health my whole view was different than when I had written the original book.

When I wrote Pressing Forward I was leading a ministry for Christian women who were struggling with anxiety and depression. The whole book was written for Christian women struggling with anxiety and depression. I wrote from a per-spective of my own story: super-spiritual - in the name of Jesus - on your face prayer - abundant scripture - non-stop worship - speak it until you receive it type of encouragement.

Although I believe in all those, my mind has broadened since the last time I touched the book - especially with working in behavioral health.

The original Pressing Forward had no room for medicine. This Pressing Forward sees how medication can be incredibly appropriate for anyone who is battling with mental health issues. I have met many honorable Christians who were on medication, or who are on medication now.

I didn't take medication during my own journey. I was offered antianxiety medication, but was too stubborn to take it for longer than five days. I really felt I was not supposed to take medication, but looking back I think I needed someone to tell me it was okay to turn to medicine. I needed permission. I wish the women in the church community around me would have been more open about medicine. I later found out that the majority of women around me were on some sort of short-term medication regimen at some point or another in their lives due to anxiety or depression. Some people do need it long term.

I'm not a medical professional but if you were to ask my permission, I would say if it's not a true chemical issue and you're considering medication - don't use the medication to numb yourself. A short-term medication regime coupled with therapy can absolutely help you.

You have options. Don't let small-minded people keep you from getting the help you need. Actually, don't let anyone tell you what is right or wrong for your life when it comes to getting proper help for your mental health.

I'm glad my first version of this book didn't make it to the market. I was one of those small-minded people.

Another thing about the previous version of this book; I spoke to you as if I had the answer for your life. I've since realized I don't know the answer for you. I don't have your answer. But you do. The other version told you what to do. This version tells you my story, in hopes that it will shake something loose in you that launches you out in your journey and helps you keep pressing forward toward living in freedom.

The original book tells you about overcoming fear as if it goes away. All that lie does is make you feel defeated when fear returns. This book tells you that fear will always be threaded into our lives. It's not necessarily a bad thing. Fear can be healthy and keep us out of harm's way.

It shouldn't be debilitating fear where your whole life is shutting down, but I want you to feel hopeful when fear comes. The presence of fear means you're onto something new. You're changing, dying a tiny death through surrender, on the verge of experiencing peace that passes all understanding. You're pressing into uncharted territory. You're letting familiar but toxic trains pass you by. You're taking a stand. You're manifesting great courage. You're pressing forward.

If fear is not protecting you or providing the fuel to launch you, it's trying to manipulate you into giving up. This is the fear that brings irrational thoughts and debilitating anxiety. This type of fear has no place in our lives.

This version of Pressing Forward meets you right where you are and says, "It's okay, friend. I see you. I understand. You're not alone. You will get through this."

I'm grateful that the publisher said I could designate my audience. I'm grateful that he said I could change my view and voice. I don't think he expected that I'd take five years' worth of work and rewrite the whole book within 30 days. Because that's exactly what I did.

I didn't need to stand on the platform and preach at you. I didn't need to pretend to have the answers. I simply needed to invite you into the intimate details of my life, bring you along for the journey and let you see the good and the bad. I needed to let you see my pain and my victories.

As I wrote this version of Pressing Forward, I imagined you as my friend, Sarah. I imagined what I would say to you if you called on me to meet for coffee. That's exactly how I've written this book - as friends sitting together and sharing our stories without judgement and cookie-cutter quick fixes. Call me weird, but that night in October of 2016, I felt the book

I had turned into publishing for review was not the book I would release. That first version was to press through finishing a long project and turning it in with the risk of rejection. I've always had a procrastination issue, which is ultimately just a control issue. I'm so stubborn about anyone telling me what to do that I won't even let myself tell me what to do. Ha!

Finishing the first version of this book and submitting it allowed me to soak my feet in the puddles of fear once again. Fear of rejection. Fear of not being good enough - only to discover that even with rejection, life still goes on.

The next version of the book - this version - was for you to read. This was always meant to be the real book. Written by the real me. Speaking directly to the heart of the real you. The first book I ever published. Despite the fear, and procrastination, and shame, and lies. This is the book that would tell my story, allowing me to speak from the perspective of my truest self.

The book, that with all my heart, I hope will encourage you to keep pressing forward.

About the Author

April Poynter has been writing creatively since she was in elementary school. As an avid blogger and freelance ghost writer, she finds joy in not just communicating with, but connecting with readers. She especially loves connecting with those that feel they live life on the fringes.

"I love the fact that blogging is so raw, that there are no rules beyond simply being honest," she says. "When people read what I write, I want them to hear my voice. I want them to laugh with me when I'm being funny, and cry with me when I'm hurting. As much as I love blogging and working on other authors' books, it has always been my dream to write my own book."

During most week days, April works with an organization that serves individuals who are battling addiction. She also owns AP Consulting, an organization that helps women with tangible next steps to start their small business.

Connect with April online at **aprilpoynter.com**.

Also Available From

WordCrafts Press

Pro-Verb Ponderings
31 Ruminations on Positive Action
by Rodney Boyd

Morning Mist
Stories from the Water's Edge
by Barbie Loflin

Why I Failed in the Music Business
and how NOT to follow in my footsteps
by Steve Grossman

Youth Ministry is Easy!
and 9 other lies
by Aaron Shaver

Chronicles of a Believer
by Don McCain

A Scarlet Cord of Hope
by Sheryl Griffin

www.wordcrafts.net

85756548R00066

Made in the USA
Lexington, KY
04 April 2018